PAVED A WAY

PAVED A WAY

INFRASTRUCTURE, POLICY, AND RACISM IN AN AMERICAN CITY

COLLIN YARBROUGH

NEW DEGREE PRESS

PAVED A WAY

INFRASTRUCTURE, POLICY, AND RACISM IN AN AMERICAN CITY

ISBN   978-1-63676-949-3 *Paperback*
       978-1-63730-015-2 *Kindle Ebook*
       978-1-63730-117-3 *Ebook*

CONTENTS

———

LAND ACKNOWLEDGEMENT

———

This book is about the occupied/unceded/stolen territory of the Caddo, Wichita, Kiowa, and Comanche who stewarded this land for nearly twelve thousand years since the Hasinai. These and other peoples experienced genocide and forced removal from the land now known as Texas. Their ancestors are present with us on this land and seek justice and healing for their people. We pay respects to elders both past and present.

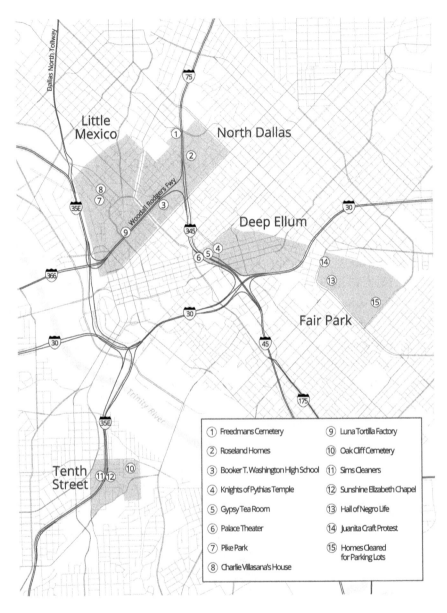

①	Freedmans Cemetery	⑨	Luna Tortilla Factory
②	Roseland Homes	⑩	Oak Cliff Cemetery
③	Booker T. Washington High School	⑪	Sims Cleaners
④	Knights of Pythias Temple	⑫	Sunshine Elizabeth Chapel
⑤	Gypsy Tea Room	⑬	Hall of Negro Life
⑥	Palace Theater	⑭	Juanita Craft Protest
⑦	Pike Park	⑮	Homes Cleared for Parking Lots
⑧	Charlie Villasana's House		

Cartography by Julie Witmer Custom Map Design,
contains information provided by the City of Dallas.

INTRODUCTION

———

My hope for the equitable future of our cities stems from an unsettling beginning.

In the spring of 2020, I wrote a paper in my master's program evaluating the design of a "large structure" here in Dallas. The list of structures I was provided with included many Dallas icons such as the Meyerson Symphony Center, the Old Red Courthouse, the Nasher Sculpture Center, and so forth. Out of the dozen or so options listed as inspiration, US 75/Central Expressway (Central) caught my eye. It seemed odd to me at first because I couldn't see the inherent value in evaluating the design of a highway.

I was very wrong.

I quickly discovered the Central I knew was actually a 1990s reconstruction and expansion of the original four- and six-lane highway built in the late 1940s, which was then lowered into the ground and widened to eight lanes in the 1990s. During construction of the lowered portion, just north of downtown Dallas, 1,157 bodies from a century-old Freedman's cemetery were relocated to make space for the new design. During the archaeological dig from 1990-94, it was discovered that the service road of the original expressway and other street modifications had paved over these formerly enslaved bodies just fifty years earlier—when archaeological protections did not exist.

I was furious. I immediately texted a classmate, "You aren't going to believe this! I'm so fucking mad!" It was a story that haunted me, and I could not let it go.

This was a highway I used *every single day.*

Thus my journey to learn about the history of the former Freedman's town began. I found a rich tapestry of stories about a tight-knit community that's practically extinct today. It used to be Black business districts filled with grocery stores, restaurants, doctors, lawyers, and theaters. It was home to activists and advocates for civil rights and opportunities for People of Color (POC) in Dallas. The same area is now home to a predominantly White, upper-class residential and bar district known as Uptown, an area I frequented in my twenties without much care or concern.

As I expanded research to other highways surrounding downtown Dallas, I found similar patterns where neighborhoods were divided, bulldozed, and/or left to decay: North Dallas, Deep Ellum, Little Mexico, Tenth Street, Fair Park, along with countless others.

It is a tangled web of infrastructure, policy, and race.

Highway development, housing crunches, inadequate city services, neighborhood displacement—it was all there. When I discuss this story about Central Expressway to Dallas natives, there is almost always a reaction along the lines of "What? I didn't know that." Now they know. Speeding down these highways my entire life, I never stopped to think about why they were built, why they were in that location, or what might have been there before.

I've come to learn Dallas is its own city, and Dallas is every city.

———

In 2019, I volunteered to help with a church luncheon. An annual event typically focused on raising money for global hunger relief, that particular year we focused on our own backyard in Dallas. One of the pieces of information passed around was a map showing they city's racial and economic segregation.[1] What I saw didn't surprise me much, as the information had been reinforced subconsciously throughout my life: Black, Latinx, and other POC live to the south and west, and people who look like me (White) live to the north and east. I am sure your hometown also has patterns.

Richard Rothstein's book, *The Color of Law*, shines a bright light on the systemic role federal policy plays in creating and perpetuating inequality through racial and economic segregation.[2] One of the most famous means of carrying this out was through the 1937 Home Owners' Loan Corporation maps, which sectioned cities along race lines, provided federally backed loans to White neighborhood and restricted access to loans in neighborhoods of color. Neighborhoods of color, given a yellow or red color on the map, were more likely to see future highway construction, housing loss, and disinvestment.[3]

1. Communities Foundation of Texas, *Dallas Economic Opportunity Assessment 2018* (Dallas, TX: Communities Foundation of Texas, 2018), 11.
2. Richard Rothstein, *The Color of Law: A Forgotten History of How Our Government Segregated America* (New York: Liveright, 2018).
3. Clayton Nall and Zachary P. O'Keeffe, *What Did Interstate Highways Do to Urban Neighborhoods?* (Stanford, CA: Stanford University, 2018), 31.

Infrastructure and policy like highways and housing maps aren't usually suitable for dinner table conversation; they're usually topics we avoid. Ironically, we feel their impact every single day. Many US cities like Detroit, Baltimore, St. Louis, Kansas City, Tampa Bay, Syracuse, and Dallas have lived or still live with the legacy of inner-city highways. This infrastructure presence contributed to the decline of urban cores, displacement of communities, and overall exacerbation of existing inequalities.

However, removing a highway, improving services, and bringing in development are not panaceas to repairing lifetimes of segregation and disenfranchisement. A changing city is often seen as a harbinger of further displacement, and communities of color see it coming from miles away. Perhaps changes like these might also serve as tools to begin dialogue, one that leads us toward a greater understanding of our cities, each other, and ourselves. As civil rights leader Rev. Peter Johnson told me, "There are no simplistic solutions."

Dallas proves to be a relevant case study for what is a larger trend of racial and economic inequality through design and policy for centuries across the United States. Federal housing policies, like redlining, exacerbated the deterioration of limited housing in segregated communities of color by not providing loans for improvements or mortgages. Affordable housing and "slum" clearance programs under the guise of "urban renewal" made it easy to clear homes surrounding the downtown area. Purchasing land for the public good through eminent domain and, further, inequitable appraisals of home's fair market value were tools used with the intent of discriminating against Black homeowners and forcing them out of areas slated for redevelopment.[4] Present-day building demolition policies are structured in such a way that predominantly Black historic districts experience greater rates of demolition than in predominantly White districts, leaving the largest intact Freedman's town in the country in a state of peril.

In my seven years as an engineer in the utility business, I learned to see how a city operates from a new vantage point: beneath the surface. Visual cues and patterns to what lay underground became key to unlocking what lay below.

Learning about Dallas's broader history has not only reshaped my point of view, but it has also called me to action in ways I could not have envisioned. This book is one of those actions. I am starting to understand the layers of my hometown both seen and unseen, recognizing new patterns in the city. When I pass an old structure, see a vacant lot, or a brand-new development, it generates a moment of pause, reflection, and meditation. I recognize new patterns, which alert me to injustice both past and present.

In many ways, I saw myself in the stories I read about engineers and planners making decisions about placing a road, highway, or park in a given community. It became easier to see the decision-making patterns and I reflected on my own complicity in perpetuating inequality. Why did I place a pipeline in one property or another? Who was impacted? Who was involved in the decision? Who was not?

A just and equitable city cannot be created with one highway removal, one policy change, or one grassroots campaign. It has taken many decades, policies, and actions to get to this

---

4.   I acknowledge these practices are prevalent today albeit in different forms and with different names, this highlights the need to understand what injustice physically looks like in our cities.

point and will take many more to repair it. As infrastructure historian Dr. Peter Norton told me, "There's good news in the sense that these frameworks [are] changing."

The road forward isn't perfect, but we all play a role.

* * *

Note: In this book, I have not *whitewashed* any of the language from Dallas's past.[5] This is intentional. In the act of revisiting history, it is important to understand the words and language used by White people to demean and control the Black, Indigenous, and People of Color (BIPOC) communities. It is not my intent to cause harm to any BIPOC readers. I want to ensure this interaction with Dallas's past is an historically and linguistically accurate account.

---

5. I am using the term Whitewashing here to refer to a practice of removing racially derogatory language to make racist history more comfortable for White people.

I

REFRAME

———

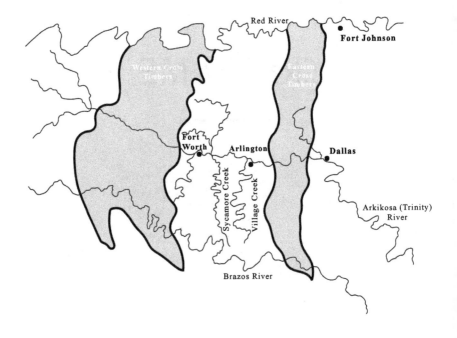

Adapted from "Republic of Texas, 1841
—Three Forks area," K. M. Shahmiri, 1989.

1

BUILT ON STOLEN LAND

———

I didn't know Dallas is built on stolen land.

Growing up here, I didn't really consider much of Dallas's history beyond the JFK assassination. Dallasites often quip that "Dallas has no reason to exist." The late Wick Allison, former owner and editor of *D Magazine*, points out that Robert Lee Thornton, Dallas's former mayor, once said, "Dallas doesn't give a damn about its history; it only cares about the future." Ironically, Allison notes, this statement was part of Thornton's presentation for Dallas's bid to be the site for the 1936 Texas Centennial at Fair Park.[6]

I didn't know about the existence of Dallas's deep history until I learned about Dallas Truth, Racial Healing & Transformation (DTRHT). DTRHT is an organization focused on "[creating] a radically inclusive city by addressing race and racism through narrative change, relationship building and equitable policies and practices."[7] A friend recommended I check out their work to learn more about the untold history

---

6. Wick Allison, "How Dallas Became Big D," *D Magazine*, September 2008.
7. "Home," Dallas Truth, Racial Healing & Transformation, accessed December 26, 2020.

of Dallas. It was a moment that fundamentally changed my life moving forward. I discovered a community vision report DTRHT published in 2019, clearly highlighting the fact Dallas is built on land stolen from the Caddo, Wichita, and other Indigenous nations.[8]

This was disorienting information to read at first. On one hand, I had some exposure to the history of Indigenous people in the United States and in Texas from my Texas public school education. On the other hand, I couldn't recall land being described as *stolen* by the settlers. Viewing the land as stolen provided a new lens for this narrative, and I found myself wondering the following question: what does it mean for my life to benefit from land stolen from Indigenous people?

DTRHT ensures the Indigenous narrative is not lost in Dallas's history or future. Jarring as it is to read the statement, it's a reminder DTRHT starts every event with and reinforces on its social media channels, encouraging others not to forget either. Being reminded Dallas is built on stolen land, with stolen people and stolen labor, pushes against the prevalent historical narratives that center colonial history around the city itself or perpetuate the myth that Dallas exists for no particular reason at all.

I continue the argument that Dallas exists precisely because it is built on the foundational racist mindset of the Republic and state of Texas.[9]

I'm offering a counternarrative.

---

8. *A New Community Vision for Dallas: 2019 Report* (Dallas, TX: Dallas Truth, Racial Healing & Transformation, 2019).

9. Ibid.

Land, Resources, and Genocide

Prehistorically, people have occupied the land now known as Texas as far back as twelve thousand years ago.[10]

One of the primary nations in north Texas, the Caddo, migrated to the area almost twelve thousand years ago. Their settlements were fairly large, sometimes containing several hundred people. A farmer and trader nation, the Caddo developed extensive trading networks between village complexes. Among other things, trade goods included salt, copper, pottery, wood, and flint.[11]

Several hundred years of colonial presence began in the 1500s with the Spanish and briefly in the 1600s with the French. The Caddo, Comanche, and Wichita were powerful traders and strategically chose their trading alliances between the French and Spanish colonial powers.[12] A peaceful acquisition of wealth developed as the Indigenous nations' skills in ranching, hunting, and farming created immense opportunity for intertribal and European trade.[13]

Disease and battling between the Europeans and the Caddo hindered the resiliency of the Indigenous strength as their land was the "bone of contention between the French and Spanish."[14] Smallpox, measles, and cholera brought by

10. Brenda B. Whorton and William L. Young, "Before John Neely Bryan," *Legacies*, (3) 2, Fall 1991, 4.
11. "American Indians: A Story Told for Thousands of Years," Bullock Museum, accessed November 10, 2020.
12. F. Todd Smith, *The Caddo Indians: Tribes at the Convergence of Empires, 1542-1854* (College Station: Texas A&M University Press, 1995), 21.
13. Smith, *The Caddo Indians*, 20.
14. Janet Claeys-Shahmiri, "Ethnohistorical Investigation of the Battle of Village Creek," (master's thesis, UTA, 1989), 23-4.

the colonial powers killed roughly 95 percent of the two hundred thousand Caddo people between the 1600s to 1800s.[15]

As the Anglo presence trickled into the land known as Texas in the 1820s, a new creed arrived as well. Historian Gary Clayton Anderson describes it as "founded on the belief that certain races of people were more accomplished and more justified in inheriting the land than were others."[16] Racism in the 1800s and a growing body of dehumanizing literature shaped Texans' view of Indigenous people, Tejanos, and Black people as wholly inferior and originating from "wretched races."[17] This racist ideology, wrapped up in southern codes of honor, required cruelty and defending the White race as a necessary component for profits, wealth, status, and "progress."[18]

With this problematic ideology, acquisition of land and owning slaves became social markers for middle-class White southerners.[19] The "everything is bigger in Texas" mentality grew from the rapid economic development fueled by cotton farming and farms, which were three times larger than the average farm across the rest of the United States.[20] Without regulations on land policies in the United States, Texas developed an identity of exceptionalism built on stolen land, stolen people, and cotton.[21]

---

15. Smith, *The Caddo Indians*, 7.
16. Gary Clayton Anderson, *The Conquest of Texas: Ethnic Cleansing in the Promised Land, 1820-1875* (Norman, OK: University of Oklahoma Press, 2005), 34.
17. Much literature about "The Indian" at this time was shaped by Thomas Jefferson's Notes on the State of Virginia, where Indigenous people were viewed as "noble savages." Anderson, *The Conquest of Texas*, 40.
18. Ibid.
19. Anderson, *The Conquest of Texas*, 39.
20. Ibid.
21. Ibid., 40.

Indigenous people stood in the way of the westward expansion of this ideology. The only option Texans saw was removal. Anderson writes, "The aggressiveness of Texans, their martial mentality and penchant for violence, their individualism and deep-seated racism, and their lust for profit made conflict with [Indigenous people] almost inevitable."[22]

Texans were battling Mexico for their independence in 1835 and did not trust the American Indians, fearing they would be enlisted and side with Mexico in the battle.[23] While some of these claims may have been true, the fear was stoked by Texas military personnel in the wake of the battles at the Alamo and San Jacinto.[24]

In 1838, the second President of the Republic of Texas, M. B. Lamar, ushered in an era professor Scott Langston says he "is comfortable calling genocide." In fact, the word *extermination* was used by Texas officials under Lamar's leadership so often that it became policy.[25] Further fueling the westward expansion, Lamar surveyed a new capital for the Republic in recognized Comanche land, in the area now known as Austin.[26]

Lamar's strict extermination policy in his administration worked to harass and persecute the American Indians, relentlessly burning their villages in the process.[27] His wars against Indigenous people, who he considered "trespassing

---

22. Ibid., 41.
23. Janet Claeys-Shahmiri, ibid., 24-5.
24. Scott Langston highlighted to me how the Alamo itself is a symbol of Spanish colonization and erasure of Indigenous culture and religion. Christianity was weaponized by Europeans and Americans to remove and destroy Indigenous people. Anderson, *The Conquest of Texas*, 108-125.
25. Anderson, *The Conquest of Texas*, 173.
26. Ibid., 174.
27. Janet Claeys-Shahmiri, ibid., 27.

vermin on Texas soil," pushed Indigenous people out of Texas, clearing the way for White settlers who were already pushing survey boundaries west.[28] Lamar spent millions on his hate-fueled war, "shooting, looting, and burning" his way westward.[29] "Why did the genocide take place?" Langston asked me. "It all goes back to land and resources."

———

The Battle of Village Creek

Groups of disparate American Indians moved westward into the Cross Timbers and Three Forks of the Arkikosa River, now known as the Trinity River.[30] This region is west of present-day Dallas in north Texas.

Historian Gary Clayton Anderson considers the Battle of Village Creek a culminating event for much of the unrest and fighting between the White settlers expanding westward and the Indigenous nations of the land. The battle is described as a "last stand," an event that drove the American Indian nations out of the Trinity River area and paved the way for White settlement in the present-day Dallas-Fort Worth metroplex.[31]

Tensions in north Texas were high as a new rash of conflicts began to occur between American Indians and newly independent Texans. Reports came into President Lamar

---

28. Ibid., 31.
29. Anderson, *The Conquest of Texas*, 191.
30. Spanish colonizer Alonso de Leon renamed the river La Santisima Trinidad in 1690.
31. Anderson, *The Conquest of Texas*, 185-194.

from many sources that the American Indians in the Three Forks of the Trinity River area were "murdering the settlers as well as stealing land from them."[32] Ironically, at this time, volunteer rangers and militia men were plundering and destroying Indigenous villages, stealing horses, pelts (animal skins), and food, which was auctioned off in Austin.[33] A fortune was to be made in the sale of stolen Indigenous goods. Anderson highlights, "[The large village on the Trinity] made up of Wichitas, Cherokees, Shawnees, Kickapoos, and Caddos, would contain considerable plunder."[34] Rewards would be great for those who enlisted.

On May 14, 1841, the 4th Brigade Texas rangers consisted of seventy volunteers from the northern Red River counties. General E. H. Tarrant gathered the rangers at Fort Johnson and headed south and west. Over five days, they traveled from near present-day Sherman, in north Texas, down into the fifteen-mile-wide wooded north-south barrier known as the lower cross timbers, in what is the eastern portion of present-day Denton county.[35]

Five days after leaving Fort Johnson, the militia entered the western cross timbers a few miles west of present-day Fort Worth. This area was the western boundary of Caddo aboriginal territory.[36] As they zigged and zagged around the cross timbers and various forks of the Trinity River, Brigadier Inspector William N. Porter reported to Texas' Secretary of War, B. T. Archer:

---

32. Janet Claeys-Shahmiri, ibid., 44.
33. Anderson, *The Conquest of Texas*, 191.
34. Ibid., 192.
35. Janet Claeys-Shahmiri, ibid., 45-46.
36. Ibid., 86.

"... we discovered tolerable fresh signs and we had every reason to believe that there were Indians in the vicinity. We soon found two of their (Indian) villages which we found to be deserted... there were some sixty or seventy lodges in these villages. [Due to their high elevation], General Tarrant deemed it imprudent to burn the villages for fear of giving alarm to the Indians... but they were in great measure destroyed with our axes."[37]

On May 24, the militia found themselves upon an inhabited village. They dropped "all manner of encumbrances," formed a line, and charged into the village on horseback, taking it swiftly by surprise.[38] After stumbling into another village about a mile from that one, the militia saw a third village nearly a mile long down the creek where they rallied back together after being scattered. When they split up again, the group led by Captain John B. Denton took fire. Several were wounded and Captain Denton was killed in the skirmish. The remainder of the militia group began to yell and make actions as if they were to storm the line.[39]

The village inhabitants retreated, and the rangers were told by an Indigenous prisoner that about half of the one thousand Native warriors from the encampment were away hunting and fighting encroaching Texans on the frontier. Realizing they would likely be outnumbered in a fight, the Texans decided to fall back. The Village Creek encampment had around 225 lodges occupied by Wichita, Cherokees, Creeks, Seminoles, Wacos, Caddos, and Kickapoos.[40] To sus-

37. "The Battle of Village Creek: The Texas Sentinel," Denton History Information, accessed November 10, 2020.

38. Ibid.

39. Janet Claeys-Shahmiri, ibid., 49.

40. Anderson, *The Conquest of Texas*, 192-3.

tain the estimated ten thousand inhabitants, approximately three hundred acres of corn were under cultivation as well. The mile-long encampment appeared to be a refuge for the fragmented nations being pushed west.[41] Tarrant's rangers stole cattle, thirty-seven horses, hundreds of pounds of lead, powder, thirty brass kettles, axes, guns, robes, and "other things not recollected."[42]

When Tarrant returned with four hundred rangers two months later in July 1841, the large encampment on Village Creek was found to be deserted.[43]

This skirmish marked the end of the safe territory on the western cross timbers for the American Indians and they began preemptively moving west for fear of further attack.[44] The ethnic cleansing was nearing completion. In October, later that year, Lamar wrote, "it is the desire of the government to have the entire western country cleared of the enemy (Indians)."[45]

Six months after the Battle of Village Creek, John Neely Bryan settled near the Elm and West forks of the Trinity River, just twenty miles east of the battle site.[46]

———

41. Ibid.
42. "The Battle of Village Creek: The Texas Sentinel," Denton History Information, accessed November 10, 2020.
43. Donald S. Frazier, "Battle of Village Creek," Texas State Historical Association Handbook of Texas, accessed November 10, 2020.
44. Anderson, *The Conquest of Texas*, 194.
45. Ibid.
46. Jackie McElhaney and Michael V. Hazel, "Dallas, TX," Texas State Historical Association Handbook of Texas, accessed February 21, 2020.

Where Do We Go from Here?

This is the beginning. Narrative change begins here.

More often than not, Dallas historical narratives start where this story ends—with John Neely Bryan. Traditional Dallas histories then move forward with a focus on the powerful White men who held significant power and privilege in setting up the city.[47] It takes significantly more effort to find any narrative of Dallas existing before that time or through a different, non-White lens.

Today, five historical markers for the Village Creek settlement and battlefield are scattered across western Arlington, about ten miles east of Fort Worth and twenty miles west of Dallas. The markers, established over the course of the twentieth century, follow the historic creek. The southernmost marker ironically sits on the seventh tee of the Lake Arlington Golf Course, just north of the Lake Arlington dam. While some sources indicate the battle may have taken place along Sycamore Creek, neighboring Village Creek to the east, there is archaeological evidence of settlements across the entire area dating back thousands of years.[48]

If you look closely, my own counternarrative falls short of humanizing oppressed Indigenous voices. The narrative centers White people and raises the oppressed only when they converge with the history of those White people, rather than Indigenous history and voices standing on their own. The Battle of Village Creek is rarely referred to in its own right but instead is recorded as part of the histories of Generals

---

47. This is a problem and my work does not yet completely remedy this shortfall in narrative change.

48. "Details for Village Creek," Texas Historic Sites Atlas, accessed November 10, 2020.

Denton and Tarrant, which are the counties home to the surrounding Denton and Fort Worth respectively. The erasure is deeply embedded.

Many of the counties in north Texas are named after captains, generals, and cabinet members involved in that battle and others: Denton, Tarrant, Archer, and Lamar. Residents of Dallas will recognize Lamar as one of the main streets running all the way from Bonton Farms and industrial areas in South Dallas, past Dallas Police Headquarters, the convention center, skyscrapers in downtown, and entertainment districts like the West End and Victory Park. It's one of the longer streets in Dallas. In January 2021, Dallas City Council unanimously approved a portion of this street to be renamed Botham Jean Boulevard, in honor of the man murdered by Dallas Police Officer Amber Guyger in 2018.[49] The renamed portion will run in front of Jean's former apartment and Dallas Police Headquarters.

A colonial narrative centered around a great White man is detrimental to the legacy of First Nations like the Caddo, Comanche, Kiowa, Kickapoo, and Wichita stewarding the land now known as north central Texas before Dallas was founded. Colonial narratives strip the value of the land down to a certain set of features deemed important from a Western perspective, leaving out the value of the Indigenous history and presence in the area dating back thousands of years, much longer than Dallas' modern history.

Acknowledging the land as stolen from Indigenous people and naming whom the land is stolen from is a good first step to moving forward. While acknowledging the Indigenous

---

49. Everton Bailey, Jr., "Dallas City Council Approves Renaming Street in Memory of Botham Jean," *Dallas Morning News*, January 13, 2021.

communities that lived and live in a particular area may be a small action, the US Department of Arts and Culture calls it "a critical public intervention, a necessary step toward honoring Native communities and enacting the much larger project of decolonization and reconciliation."[50]

The Native Governance Center provides a framework for creating land acknowledgements:

- Self-reflection: Why am I doing a land acknowledgement? Is this to inspire action or *because everyone is doing it?*
- Do homework: Research Indigenous people to whom the land belongs, the history of the land and related treaties, Indigenous place names and language, names of Indigenous people from these communities, etc.
- Use appropriate language: Do not sugarcoat the past. Terms like genocide, ethnic cleansing, stolen land, and forced removal accurately reflect colonial actions.
- Use past, present, and future tenses: Indigenous people are still here and thriving.
- Land acknowledgements shouldn't be grim: Acknowledgements are a living celebration of Indigenous communities. How am I leaving Indigenous people in a stronger, more empowered place because of this land acknowledgement?[51]

50. USDAC is not a government entity, it is a grassroots network shaping a culture of empathy, equity, and belonging. "Honor Native Land: A Guide and Call to Acknowledgment," U.S. Department of Arts and Culture, accessed February 21, 2021.
51. "A Guide to Indigenous Land Acknowledgment," Native Governance Center, accessed February 21, 2021.

Professor Scott Langston calls on us to increase our Native American literacy rate. "Our knowledge and understanding of Native peoples is almost nonexistent and are filled with stereotypes, and that creates problems," he says. The system is designed to silence and erase Indigenous voices.

Acknowledgement is a first step in the journey of unpacking the ways our cities are built with systems of power and erasure, not only of Indigenous voices but of all Black, Indigenous, and People of Color (BIPOC) voices. The framework above is a guide that can mobilize individual and collective action toward elevating marginalized voices. True reconciliation requires acknowledgement and acceptance of past injustice.

In that journey, we are only at the beginning.

2

THE CENTRAL ARGUMENT

———

Before I crossed the threshold of Dallas's Freedman's Cemetery, I was cleansed by sage, bowed my head, and put on my mask. This was the first time I stepped into the hallowed space. Driving past the cemetery throughout my early twenties on my way to the Uptown bar district, I don't recall ever paying much attention to it. Perhaps this is due to the fact that the space looks like an open grassy park. Or maybe I was too preoccupied with whatever was going on in my own life to consider my hometown's history.

It's possible I considered the Freedman's Cemetery just another part of Greenwood Cemetery to the southwest; Greenwood bordered the building one of my friends lived in, and I parked on the street between the cemetery and the building several times. I remember thinking on more than one occasion, "Why the heck is there a cemetery in the middle this brand new development? Who would put that here?"

A few years later, in 2020, I learned the question I needed to ask was closer to "Why did we put apartments here?" Only recently, did I learn there are four separate historic cemeteries in the area—Protestant, Catholic, Jewish, and Black—and that they all predate the apartments.

The Black cemetery, known locally as the Freedman's Cemetery, is considered one of the largest freedmen's cemeteries in the United States: cemeteries where freed slaves and their descendants are buried. Over the past 150 years, Freedman's Cemetery has seen at least three iterations of infrastructure development disruption: the Houston & Texas Central (H&TC) railroad, the construction of Central Expressway, and the reconstruction and widening of Central Expressway.

The H&TC railroad laid the original path next to the cemetery in 1872. It's estimated the original construction of Central Expressway in the 1940s, wider than the boundary of the H&TC tracks, paved over existing graves, headstones and all.[52] Oral history suggests headstones and other grave materials were mixed in with the construction fill. When Central began a widening project forty years later, in order to meet traffic demands, Black Dallasites like Drs. Robert Prince and Mamie McKnight advocated for the cemetery, ensuring the expansion did not repeat history.[53] In 1994, $12 million and four years of archaeological digging later, 1,157 bodies were relocated and reinterred further west in the cemetery, making space for the highway development.[54]

As I stood in the early summer Dallas heat, I couldn't imagine worse terms for my first visit to the Freedman's

52. James M. Davidson, "An Archival History of Freedman's Cemetery, Dallas, Texas," in *Freedman's Cemetery*, eds. Duane E. Peter, Marsha Prior, Melissa M. Green, and Victoria G. Clow (Plano, Texas: Geo-Marine, Inc., 2000), 45.

53. Duane E. Peter, "The Freedman's Cemetery Project," in *Freedman's Cemetery*, eds. Duane E. Peter, Marsha Prior, Melissa M. Green, and Victoria G. Clow (Plano, Texas: Geo-Marine, Inc., 2000), 5.

54. Ibid., 7.

cemetery to take place. I gathered with about three hundred other people for a prayer vigil the weekend after George Floyd was publicly murdered by police officer Derek Chauvin in Minneapolis. I was hopeful that we might be at a new groundswell of broad support for racial equity as a nation; however, any optimism was tempered by the feeling I had walking the grounds. The roar of the highway was inescapable; prayers shouted through a bullhorn fought to be heard over the din of cars speeding through the canyon adjacent to the cemetery. I leaned over to my partner and sighed, "I guess not all bodies get to rest in peace."

It's true. While the bodies were properly exhumed and relocated during the highway widening, many questions about human ideals still haunt the space. We valued the development of infrastructure over the peace and dignity of human life and afterlife. What decisions were made to place these pieces of infrastructure along these particular alignments? What factors were at play for the common good? Who was involved in those processes?

———

Freedman's Town Beginnings

Texas harbored slaveholders prior to the Civil War, due to the former Republic's positive stance on slavery and restriction of rights for free Blacks.[55] Prior to the start of the Civil War conflict, 76 percent of the slave owners in Dallas County

---

55. Alwyn Barr, *Black Texans: A History of Negroes in Texas, 1528-1971* (Austin: Jenkins Pub. Co., 1973), Ch. 1-2.

were born in Kentucky, Tennessee, Virginia, or the Carolinas.[56] News of emancipation for slaves reached Texas on June 19, 1865. In 1869, when much of Dallas was still open land, freedmen came to Dallas in search of better economic opportunities and purchased one-acre lots just northeast of the city limits.[57] Freedmen, represented by Sam Eakins, purchased an acre of land from William H. Boales for twenty-five dollars to serve as a burial ground.[58]

The freedmen community spanned from present-day Uptown to the downtown Arts District. In 1872, a few years after Freedman's Town was founded, the H&TC railroad came through Dallas on its way to St. Louis after significant coaxing from local White business leaders. The Central tracks cut through the eastern half of Freedman's Town and just past the eastern edge of the cemetery in 1872. Railroad construction fueled a boom as homes were built up alongside the tracks and new job opportunities abounded for Black Dallasites.

Due to various forms of segregation, self-sufficiency was a necessity for Black residents in Dallas and it also allowed for greater control over their own environment.[59] Freedman's Town built shops and offered services to care for the community. These business corridors primarily occupied Hall

56. Thomas H. Smith, "African Americans in Dallas: From Slavery to Freedom," in *Dallas Reconsidered: Essays in Local History*, edited by Michael V. Hazel (Dallas: Three Forks Press, 1995), 125.

57. Marsha Prior and Robert V. Kemper, "From Freedman's Town to Uptown," *Urban Anthropology and Studies of Cultural Systems and World Economic Development* 34, no. 2/3 (Summer-Fall 2005), 179.

58. James M. Davidson, ibid., 21.

59. To be clear, I am not advocating that segregation is a social good. This environment was still shrouded within the confines of a White dominated power structure and restricted civil rights. I am attempting to elevate the residents as active resistors to the oppression of segregation.

and Cochran Streets, on the northeastern edge of present day downtown Dallas. There were churches, schools, black-smiths, meat markets, as well as professional trades such as doctors and lawyers. It was a vibrant community that served the needs that were left unmet by the surrounding metropolis. In 1889, the City of Dallas officially renamed the area "North Dallas."[60]

Make Dallas Beautiful

At the same time, around 1900, Dallas found itself attempt-ing to manage growth and maintain its identity as a beauti-ful and prosperous city. What resulted was haphazard: the downtown area had three street grids of different orienta-tions attempting to merge together in what looks like a spider web made up of streets.[61] Historian William H. Wilson notes that "Dallas suffered from other deficiencies—bureaucratic, esthetic, and recreational... The city lacked a boulevard sys-tem. Few residential streets or neighborhoods were designed for stability and long-term value. In short, Dallas was chok-ing on its own growth."[62] In a style emblematic of things to come, Dallas's White business leadership stepped in to promote strategies they deemed best for the city as a whole.

---

60. Marsha Prior and Robert V. Kemper, ibid., 181-82.
61. Orientation of street grids differed due to some streets being aligned with the Trinity River and some streets being organized on a N-E-S-W grid.
62. William H. Wilson, "Adapting to Growth: Dallas, Texas and the Kessler Plan, 1908-1933," *Arizona and the West* 25, no. 3 (Autumn 1983), 247-8.

One of those leaders, George B. Dealey, operating officer and later owner of the *Dallas Morning News* (*DMN*), stepped up to the task. The City of Dallas had already attempted a Civic Improvement League, creating a program of parks and planning that was ultimately defeated. In an effort to maintain momentum, Dealey utilized the power of the *DMN* to run syndicated and original articles about the need for civic beauty and the City Beautiful movement.[63]

Wilson describes the City Beautiful ideology as stressing comprehensive planning centered around park and boulevard systems. It highlighted that buildings and public spaces should be both practical and visually appealing. What attracted Dealey, and Dallas's White business leadership, was the success of the movement within cities (e.g., Chicago, Baltimore, San Francisco) commanding strong local involvement of private enterprise and commitments to civic pride.[64] The flowing San Antonio Riverwalk, with the river built up with walkways on either side and shopping through the downtown area, is a prime example of City Beautiful in action. For a city concerned with self-image and attempting to wrangle growth, this felt like a winning strategy.

New Visions

In 1910, Dealey encouraged the newly formed Chamber of Commerce to bring J. Horace McFarland, a key figure of

---

63. Ibid., 250.
64. Ibid., 246.

30 · PAVED A WAY

the City Beautiful movement, to speak to Dallas business leaders. The members were inspired enough that an adjunct committee was formed, the City Plan and Improvement League (CPIL). The CPIL was to work with city officials in developing a comprehensive plan for the city, and its first move was to bring the famed landscape architect George Kessler to Dallas.[65]

Kessler met with park board and municipal commission officials during his trip to Dallas. In his report released in 1912, Kessler noted Dallas struggled from the difficulties of expansion with "no apparent thought having been given in the interim to the needs of the increasing population."[66] He further highlights the physical boundaries choking and directing growth in Dallas: the Trinity River to the west, the Texas & Pacific (T&P) railroad to the north, rail yards to the south, and the H&TC railroad to the east. Kessler painted these pieces of infrastructure as a literal and figurative chokehold on Dallas.

Kessler's thoughts on freeing up the city for growth fell on removing as many barriers as possible. In line with what the CPIL was hoping for from the plan, levees and flood control were at the top of his list. Kessler called for levees a quarter mile wide and twenty-five feet high along the Trinity. He envisioned the Trinity would become more of a center to the city and that planning efforts must take care in ensuring the western lands were given equal consideration if Dallas was to survive future growth beyond one hundred thousand residents.[67]

One other hallmark of Kessler's 1911 plan was the comprehensive boulevard and parks system. These boulevards were

---

65. Ibid., 250-51.

66. George Kessler, *A City Plan for Dallas* (Dallas: Dallas Park and Recreation Department, 1911), 7.

67. Ibid., 10-11

designed to link together a comprehensive parks system. Kessler relayed that "if the majority of people are to have the full benefit of outdoor recreation, parks and playgrounds must be provided within easy walking distance of their homes."[68] Access to outdoor space was a novel idea at the time and is still a battleground issue in major metropolitan areas today.

It is encouraging to see emphasis on the well-being of the people in the city over one hundred years ago, rather than a pure drive to promote industry and business at all costs. The critical question we must ask is: did Kessler intend that well-being to extend to all residents or just the residents who looked like him? Kessler's park system was to be connected by roads encircling the city, linking with boulevards. The boulevards were designed to increase the value of the land around them and provide a pleasurable experience while driving and be attractive to the onlooker. Parkways generally followed the flow of creeks, and boulevards would have a split driveway with a wide, grassy median.

Freeing up the western edge of Dallas through levees and channelization, Kessler turned his focus toward the railroads crisscrossing the city.[69] In order to free up space and create a safer urban environment, he called for the elimination of numerous railroad stations and tracks in the downtown area, for two belt line railroads to encircle Dallas, West Dallas, and Oak Cliff (suburbs west and south of the central city).

Meanwhile, North Dallas continued to grow within the segregated confines of these broader city plans. Municipal ordinances at the time dictated the resident color of a street,

---

68. Ibid., 25.

69. Channelization is the process of deepening and widening a river to increase flow, resulting in less damage to banks.

either Black or White, maintaining control of the use of land before official zoning ordinances were in place.[70]

In the 1920s, there was an increased desire by Black residents to live in North Dallas, gaining access to opportunities there and a chance to get out of sharecropping.[71] This led to an influx of residents into the community. The mixed-use nature of North Dallas, with businesses and dwellings intermingled with each other, made the area an attractive place to live for Black Dallasites.

An array of doctors, clothing stores, taxi services, theaters, drug stores, dry cleaners, and a number of beauty parlors filled the Hall Street and Thomas Avenue Black business district.[72] The Pinkston Clinic provided crucial medical services to Dallas's Black community and, in later years, The Empire Room hosted live entertainers like Ray Charles.[73]

Housing and a Highway

An increasing population, coupled with a lack of housing options for Black Dallasites, created a difficult situation for the racially landlocked North Dallas community. From an outsider's perspective, overcrowding, poverty, and deterioration

---

70. Darwin Payne, *Quest for Justice: Louis A. Bedford Jr. and the Struggle for Equal Rights in Texas* (Dallas: Southern Methodist University Press, 2009), 21.

71. Sharecropping is a type of farming where families rent land from a landowner in return for a share of the crops produced on the land. This is often considered another form of slavery. Darwin Payne, Quest for Justice, 20.

72. Marsha Prior and Robert V. Kemper, ibid., 184-85.

73. Darwin Payne, *Quest for Justice*, 27.

defined North Dallas.[74] In a 1924 housing survey, carried out by Elmer Scott, a prominent social welfare advocate, we begin to see some of the effects that lack of access to public services can have. Half of the buildings in North Dallas did not have gas, electricity, or running water. One in five homes in the area was considered "uninhabitable."[75]

At this time, in the late '20s and early '30s, public housing programs started popping up across the United States. The Housing Act of 1937 enacted the first federal public housing program, emphasizing the importance of slum clearance in the process. The law required a one-to-one removal of slum housing to new housing provided. The rhetoric equating slums to "cancer" was used to elevate the importance of wholesale slum removal in order to save the urban cores of cities, while simultaneously equating Black residents with disease.[76] Despite a relatively positive widespread appeal for the construction of public housing, the disparities were often stacked against the Black community.

In Dallas, funding was approved in 1935, through the Public Works Administration, for the first White and Black housing projects. Cedar Springs, the White project, was the first to be built. Construction of Cedar Springs occurred on empty land, allowing for housing to be built before clearing was required. Money ran out in the attempts to find and purchase a site for the Black project due to the difficulty in determining ownership rights on parcels of land. Four years

---

74. Marsha Prior and Robert V. Kemper, ibid., 185-86.

75. Ibid., 186.

76. Robert B. Fairbanks, *The War on Slums in the Southwest: Public Housing and Slum Clearance in Texas, Arizona, and New Mexico, 1935-1965* (Philadelphia: Temple University Press, 2014), 47-48.

later, with new funding from the 1937 act, the first Black housing project began construction.[77]

The Roseland Homes project was proposed to be built east of the H&TC tracks in North Dallas, referred to by residents as their "Highland Park."[78] Homeowners in the area protested the development of the project, because it would remove one of "the largest [concentrations] of owner-occupied dwellings within Freedman's Town/North Dallas... a severe interruption in the communal order of the enclave..."[79] Development of the Roseland project in 1942 required the removal of several hundred homes and replaced them with 650 new rental units.[80] Even with the additional housing units from Roseland Homes, the neighborhood still saw a loss of 450 housing units between 1940-50.[81]

The subsequent Housing Acts of 1949 and 1954 built on the slum clearance program through the development of what was termed "urban renewal." While discussing this with Dr. Marvin Dulaney, the deputy director of the African American Museum of Dallas, he asked me, quoting James Baldwin, "You know what urban renewal really meant? Negro removal."

Amid battles with the railroad to remove the tracks and two world wars causing machinery and steel shortages, the City of Dallas and Texas Highway Commission were delayed

77. Ibid., 41.

78. Highland Park is a small city in the middle of Dallas nearly exclusively made up of wealthy White residents living in nicely kept homes of Black Dallas. Robert B. Fairbanks, *The War on Slums in the Southwest*, 40-43, 64.

79. Terry Anne Schulte and Marsha Prior, "Epilogue," in *Freedman's Cemetery*, eds. Duane E. Peter, Marsha Prior, Melissa M. Green, and Victoria G. Clow (Plano, Texas: Geo-Marine, Inc., 2000), 194.

80. Darwin Payne, *Quest for Justice*, 37.

81. U.S. Census Bureau, "Characteristics of Housing by Census Tracts: 1950," Dallas, Texas Tables, 1950, table 2, accessed July 15, 2020. Marsha Prior and Robert V. Kemper, "From Freedman's Town to Uptown," 193.

until the 1940s before beginning design and construction of Central Boulevard. The northern section would replace the path of the Central tracks north from Main Street in downtown Dallas and connect to major cross streets on the journey north. The southern section would instead parallel the Central tracks through South Dallas, leaving the railway in operation.[82]

The space originally proposed for the boulevard meant nearby property owners would be displaced to clear the one-hundred-foot right-of-way. Similar to Roseland Homes, eminent domain laws gave residents little recourse to challenge the appraised value of their homes and businesses.[83] A lack of Black representation and involvement in the planning and design processes only exacerbated the disenfranchisement of communities like North Dallas and resulted in "inadequate reparations" as residents received below market values from the City for their property.[84]

The *Dallas Express* reported the anguish and frustration North Dallas residents felt:

> "Questions are coming fast and furious from the many long time residents who must move as their homes must be torn down to make way for the Central Boulevard expressway. Where are we going? What are we going to do?… What of my family?… The city has stated that October 15th (1946) is the final date for occupancy for a section that houses 1,500 persons. With

82. Allen Quinn, "Central Boulevard Cost Total Put at 18 Millions," *Dallas Morning News*, August 24, 1947.

83. Marsha Prior and Robert V. Kemper, "From Freedman's Town to Uptown," 191.

84. Terry Anne Schulte and Marsha Prior, "Epilogue," 192.

winter just a few months away, their eviction notice just a few days away, no place available for them to rent and no housing construction for Negroes underway, these persons are facing a crucial time… Many of the inhabitants are lifelong residents of their particular homes. Their homes are living symbols of their life-long struggles and have been in their families for generations."[85]

A 1925 update on progress of the Kessler Plan appeared to indicate this was exactly the desired effect of the new boulevard. "This plan would make [Central] one of the finest in the United States, and property now utilized for cheap industrial purposes or negro residential districts would be changed into high-class apartment and retail business districts."[86] This prediction would come true seventy-five years later, confirming Dr. Dulaney's comment.

The construction of Central finally began in the late 1940s, and the name was changed from Central Boulevard to Central *Expressway*. The new term signified "speed rather than pleasure driving" and vowed to "save thousands of local motorists five to fifteen minutes in driving to or from work."[87] The value of saving a marginal amount of time on other people's commutes was enough to justify cutting through the heart of a neighborhood.

The research shows an interesting design inversion from the proposed Kessler Plan. High demand and usage of

85. "Central Boulevard to Take in Homes of Long-Time Residents," *Dallas Express*, October 5, 1946.

86. Louis P. Head, *The Kessler City Plan for Dallas: A Review of the Plan and Progress on Its Accomplishment* (Dallas: Dallas Morning News, 1925), 14.

87. "Central Expressway Readied for Opening," *Dallas Morning News*, July 28, 1949.

automobiles fueled a road building boom in the mid-twentieth century, placing the value of automobiles over most anything else in roadway designs. For example, the addition of lanes is a common refrain for reducing traffic rather than modifying the roadway to accommodate other modes of transportation (buses, bikes, walking, etc.). The new expressway design called for three twelve-foot main lanes and frontage roads in either direction as you got closer to downtown and two lanes in either direction further north. This design stood in stark contrast to the tree-lined and pedestrian-focused boulevard Kessler originally envisioned for Dallas.

Central Expressway was the first of its kind in Texas and signaled a new barrier in the North Dallas neighborhood. What was once an easy traverse across the Central tracks now stood as a literal and figurative wall confining the community.[88]

———

In the African American History Museum, there hangs a photo of children in a fifth-grade class at B. F. Darrell Elementary, the only Black elementary school in Dallas at the time, situated just east of Central and Hall Street. Students at the school were tasked with a project to build a model of what the new expressway would look like through their neighborhood. The caption on the photo describes how the children were depicting Central coming through the neighborhood and the Hall Street overpass projecting above the board. How would you like a six-lane highway to cut through your neighborhood?

---

88. Terry Anne Schulte and Marsha Prior, "Epilogue," 192.

Once the actual highway was complete, children had to walk under the Hall Street overpass, or attempt crossing six lanes of highway and four lanes of frontage roads in morning traffic in order to get to school.[89] Businesses once occupying Hall Street were either eliminated in the construction or hampered from further development.[90] It was a far cry from the connected roadway and park system Kessler had proposed nearly forty years earlier. The dream of meandering parks and roads gave way to the priorities of the automobile, and communities in the path bore the majority of the losses associated with that progress.

Once, Twice, Three Times

While the rest of Dallas boomed, the Black North Dallas community went into free fall. Staggering population and housing loss occurred in North Dallas during the forty years following the construction of the Roseland Homes project and Central Expressway. North Dallas had a population of 15,780 African Americans and 5,505 housing units according to the 1940 census records.[91] By 1980, those numbers dropped to 1,531 and 998, respectively.[92]

A loop of highways around downtown continued to build out over the next few decades, bisecting the heart of North

89. Ibid.

90. Marsha Prior and Robert V. Kemper, ibid., 192.

91. Ibid., 193.

92. U.S. Census Bureau, "Characteristics of Housing by Census Tracts: 1950," Dallas, Texas Tables, 1950, table 2, accessed July 15, 2020.

Dallas. Completion of the depressed east-west Woodall Rodgers Freeway in the 1980s separated Booker T. Washington High School from what was left of the North Dallas community to the north. The freeway also erased the Dunbar Library, the first library for African Americans in Dallas, and several churches in preparing the land for construction.[93]

A 1982 comprehensive plan developing a vision of Dallas in the year 2000 no longer listed North Dallas as a neighborhood—it was instead included as part of "Oak Lawn," a predominantly White neighborhood to the west.[94]

Traffic demand on Central quickly caught up to capacity and became a hotly contested issue in the City of Dallas during the '70s and '80s. Proposals between the City and state officials, business leaders, and citizen groups went in circles for years before agreeing to redevelop Central into an eight-lane lowered highway.

Part of that expansion would require additional right-of-way through former North Dallas, including land in Freedman's Cemetery, which officially closed in 1907.[95] The City later turned the cemetery into a memorial park with a playground in 1965, with a granite marker being the only reference to the past and present life as a cemetery.[96] As the Texas Department of Transportation (TXDOT) began archaeological studies for acquiring property to expand Central in 1985, no members of Dallas's Black community were notified or even part of the process for several more years.[97]

---

93. Terry Anne Schulte and Marsha Prior, ibid., 196.
94. Marsha Prior and Robert V. Kemper, ibid., 197.
95. Duane E. Peter, "The Freedman's Cemetery Project," 3.
96. James M. Davidson, ibid., 45.
97. Duane E. Peter, ibid., 4-5.

During the late '80s, significant redevelopment of the North Dallas area and disturbance of remains was increasing public awareness of the cemetery.[98]

Dr. Mamie McKnight, then president of Black Dallas Remembered, filed a 1989 petition with the Environmental Studies Section of TXDOT advocating on behalf of former North Dallas residents and descendants buried in the cemetery. She was "interested in knowing the impact any proposed plans for highway expansion or massive transit systems (DART was planning underground rail at the time) may have on [the] burial ground. It appear[ed] that portion of the cemetery [was] already covered by existing streets."[99]

Community representatives wanted to ensure the same erasure toward their ancestors did not happen again.

Compromise was found two years later between TXDOT and Black Dallas Remembered, allowing for the "sensitive removal and reinternment of graves within the proposed right-of-way, and the eventual clearance for the expansion of North Central Expressway."[100] Archaeological digs and reinternment of 1,157 bodies would take longer than anyone ever anticipated, spanning four years. The unprecedented coalition between the Black community and state and local agencies led to the preservation of Black memory and contributions to the building of Dallas.[101] However, before long, many of the physical reminders of that history would be gone forever.

Simultaneously with the redevelopment of Central Expressway, the City of Dallas created the Uptown Public

98. Ibid.
99. Ibid.
100. Ibid.
101. Ibid.

Improvement District (PID) in 1993 to cover the area formerly known as North Dallas.[102] This PID is charged with redeveloping the areas near the cemeteries, the new historic State Thomas district, and areas north of downtown and Woodall Rogers Freeway.[103] Tax and investment dollars were now available to turn the nearly vacant land into a freshly built community.

Entering the 2000s, Uptown looked much as it does today with wall-to-wall condominiums and apartments and a demographic makeup of predominantly middle- and upper-class White people. The expanded and renovated Booker T. Washington High School, St. Paul United Methodist Church, and Moorland YMCA remain some of the only North Dallas structures in the newly redeveloped downtown Arts District, space formerly occupying North Dallas' southern border.[104] Standing among the modern concert halls and museums, these structures stand in defiance of the city that has worked so hard to erase Black history.

It has taken generations for the built environment in many of our cities and towns to be where they are today, and we cannot forget that as we move about in our daily lives. When I drive down Central or Woodall, it's nearly impossible for me not to think about what stood on the ground beneath and surrounding the highways. That's often where the journey of reframing our history begins. It's an acknowledgement that something else existed and we now hold space

---

102. Like a glorified Home Owners Association, a Public Improvement District is an additional tax levied on an area used for neighborhood specific improvements like safety, trash clean up, etc. "Uptown PID," City of Dallas Office of Economic Development, accessed October 1, 2020.

103. Marsha Prior and Robert V. Kemper, ibid., 207.

104. Ibid., 197.

for both the past and the present simultaneously. They are not necessarily in conflict with each other, but they inform each other. Much like a land acknowledgement pulls us back into the space that was and is native, our built forms serve as an acknowledgement of past decisions.

With acknowledgement, we continue the journey of healing injustice.

3

DEEP ELLUM BLUES

———

I grew up with the vague sense Deep Ellum was not a place I should go; that it was a place to be avoided. My mind associated the area with nightclubs, crime, and live music. I'm sure this was largely due to the narrative I heard in the news growing up. I remember hearing about murders and other crimes in Deep Ellum—they were the only references I had of the area. My preconceived notions about the neighborhood were shaped by those stories.

Alternatively, I also heard tons of commercials on the radio for live music venues in Deep Ellum like Trees and Club Dada, a prime venue choice for Booker T. Washington graduates like the members of Edie Brickell & New Bohemians.[105] One thing is for certain: Deep Ellum's history and role at the epicenter of music and nightlife in Dallas has never been contested.

However, Deep Ellum's history runs a little deeper than bars, blues, and crime. It was, and still is in many ways, a

———

105. Alaena Hostetter, "Club Dada Celebrates 30 Years as Deep Ellum's Artistic Backbone," *Dallas Observer*, September 19, 2016.

place in Dallas where different worlds collided—a sort of "alternate reality," as historian Alan Govenar describes it. It is a reality born at the intersection of transportation and race.

––––––

A Railroad Crossroads

As the frontier grew in the post-Civil War era, the city vied for major railroad routes to furiously lay track across the United States. Two railroads in particular, the H&TC and the Texas & Pacific (T&P), were making their way across Texas in the 1860s to 1870s.[106] Neither railroad was originally designed to pass directly through Dallas.

The H&TC originally began north from Galveston in 1859, with hopes of shortening the four-week journey by wagon between Houston and Dallas—the two largest trading hubs in the state. Ending in St. Louis, Missouri, the H&TC connected the railroad to the eastern half of United States.[107]

White citizens of Dallas sprang into action when they learned the railroad was originally planned to run eight miles east of the city. Losing out on a railroad connection would have impacted the ease of trading and facilitating commerce. William Henry Gaston, former Confederate army officer turned banker and major landowner, donated land for the H&TC right-of-way to pass through the east side of town. Sweetening the pot, Gaston and other White businessmen

––––––

106. Jackie McElhaney, "From Oxen to Rails: The Development of Dallas as a Transportation Center," *Legacies*: A History Journal for Dallas and North Central Texas 7, no. 1 (Spring, 1995): 14.

107. Ibid., 8.

raised five thousand dollars, roughly one hundred thousand in present value, and the City agreed to extend the Elm, Main, and Commerce Streets eastward to ease the commute to the railroad and facilitate commerce.[108]

The first H&TC steamer rolled into Dallas on July 16, 1872 carrying a load of lumber and one passenger car.[109] The city exploded with excitement. John Milton McCoy, the first city attorney for Dallas, wrote his brother in Indianapolis, "Everything points to the crossing of two great roads here. Property is at exorbitant prices. The people are crazy, talking about Dallas being the Indianapolis of Texas for a railroad center. Emigration pouring in and everybody talking about the town."[110] Dallas had situated itself to become the first railroad crossroads in Texas.

Congress chartered the T&P railroad in 1871, originally planning to run it east-west along the thirty-second parallel. This would place the path about fifty miles south of Dallas, between Marshall, Texas, and San Diego, California. A local Texas legislator snuck a rider in the bill requiring the new railroad to be within a mile of Browder Springs, Dallas's water supply.[111] Needless to say, this didn't sit well with the T&P when it found out, and it subsequently threatened to bypass Dallas altogether.

Rescuing this railroad opportunity as well, Gaston offered up 142 acres for the right-of-way and ten acres for a station. Meanwhile, the City of Dallas ponied up two

108. Alan Govenar and Jay Brakefield, *Deep Ellum: The Other Side of Dallas* (College Station: Texas A&M University Press, 2013), 31.
109. Jackie McElhaney, "From Oxen to Rails," 14.
110. *When Dallas Became a City: Letters of John Milton McCoy, 1870-1881*, edited by Elizabeth York Enstam (Dallas: Dallas Historical Society, 1982), 46-47.
111. Govenar and Brakefield, *Deep Ellum*, 32.

hundred thousand dollars—roughly $4.2 million in present value—in bonds and another five thousand in cash. City officials also promised to rename the street the tracks would run down as "Pacific." Together, this was enough incentive for the railroad to stay the course through Dallas. By February 1873, T&P trains began making their way to the intersection with the north-south H&TC tracks.[112]

Harlem in Miniature

Not only did the railroads fuel economic growth for White business interests in Dallas, but they fueled opportunity for Dallas' Black community as well. Dallas historian A. C. Green notes, "Dallas became a mecca for [formerly enslaved people], and several freedmen's towns... sprung up on its outskirts."[113] Three areas began to spring up along the H&TC tracks: the North Dallas freedmen's town, Stringtown, and Deep Ellum.

Deep Ellum's hub was near the intersection of the railroads east of downtown, primarily the H&TC tracks, known as Central Track, and Elm Street. North Dallas grew to the north and west of Deep Ellum, connected by the Central Track. The railroads brought jobs for Black men, and soon the Stringtown community began to build shotgun houses along the tracks between the two neighborhoods. Urban legends say shotgun houses get their name because you could shoot a shotgun shell from the front door to the back door and not

112. Ibid.

113. A. C. Greene, *Dallas USA* (Austin: Texas Monthly Press, 1984), 63.

hit anything; they are generally long, narrow, single story homes with a front room, a middle room, and a kitchen.[114]

"[Housing development in Deep Ellum] was interesting to me from a kind of urban design standpoint," Alan Govenar, co-author of *Deep Ellum: The Other Side of Dallas*, told me. "It was very much like a West African village." Having worked in West Africa himself, Govenar recalled the "shotgun house is something [that originated in] in West Africa and is an African kind of vernacular architecture."

The new Stringtown and Central Track residents designed and built a community around their own context in spite of the strictures of a segregated metropolis. Within these communities, Dallas began to see the first de facto (by common practice) housing segregation.

Alan called my attention to the 1911 Negro Business Directory, which I remembered looking at while visiting the African American Museum at Fair Park. Black businesses in the directory showed they were originally spread across downtown Dallas. Only after "separate but equal" principles rippled from the 1896 United States Supreme Court decision in *Plessy v. Ferguson* did this relatively integrated business network begin to change. Dallas was late to the official segregation game and developed a segregation ordinance in 1916, codifying segregation and pushing Black businesses out of downtown Dallas.[115]

While White Dallas was attempting to restrict Black space, Black Dallasites were constructing it. That same year, 1916, the Knights of Pythian Temple opened in Deep Ellum. The Pythian Grand Lodge hired William Sidney Pittman,

---

114. Govenar and Brakefield, *Deep Ellum*, 36.
115. Ibid., 47.

son-in-law to Booker T. Washington and Dallas's first Black architect, to design the building and Black contractor W. C. White to build their new lodge.[116] Eventually, the Knight of Pythias would have nearly thirty-five thousand members in Texas, surpassing even the Black Masons.[117] Pittman's Pythian Temple served as a meeting place for the fraternal order, as well as a home to a drugstore, dentists, barbers, and other professionals.[118]

Black businesses began taking root along Central Track, replacing shotgun houses in Stringtown. A strong Black corridor developed along Central Track while the Elm Street corridor remained mostly White and Jewish. However, the Jewish business owners on Elm served both White and Black communities.[119] Pawn Shops in Deep Ellum were almost exclusively Jewish-owned and "operated as [banks] by lending money and giving credit and selling merchandise at reasonable prices."[120] Families like the Goldsteins, Feldmans, and Wilonskys owned shops over the decades, some as late as 1997.[121]

Deep Ellum was one of the few places in Dallas where it was acceptable for people of different skin colors to be in community together, and thus was also one of the few places Dallas's Black community could shop. In fact, Deep Ellum was such a hot Black commercial district that some called

116. Carol Roark, "The Story of the Pythian Temple," *Legacies: A History Journal for Dallas and North Central Texas* 29, no. 1 (Spring 2017): 7,9.

117. Alwyn Barr, *Black Texans: A History of African Americans in Texas, 1528-1995* (Norman: University of Oklahoma Press, 1996), 167.

118. In 2017, the building was added to the National Register of Historic Landmarks and in 2020 was restored as a boutique hotel within a mixed use development. Carol Roark, "The Story of the Pythian Temple," Legacies, 10.

119. Govenar and Brakefield, *Deep Ellum*, 36.

120. Ibid., 72.

121. Ibid., 76.

it the Black Downtown, Black Fifth Avenue, and even Harlem in Miniature. Dallas's first Black judge, Louis Bedford, described the importance of Deep Ellum like this:

> "[Deep Ellum] was centrally located. So, since people came from every direction… you didn't have shopping centers and all the satellite places to go; it was right down there. So, it seems logical to me that if Whites had a downtown section that was convenient for everyone, Blacks would need the same thing… If they wanted to have a bite to eat and they had no place to eat because of the segregated atmosphere, there was Deep Ellum. They had to go to the restroom, there was Deep Ellum. It was someplace central where people could go. It was the heart. There were people living in Oak Cliff, people living in South Dallas, people living in North Dallas, but Deep Ellum was the core."[122]

Deep Ellum Nightlife

No one is exactly sure when the Deep Ellum name came into existence, but everyone agrees on the phonetic origin.

Elm Street was considered a main street in Dallas and was the furthest extension east of the street away from downtown. The "deep" connotation was used to describe that it was far away from the city center, while "ellum" was the

---

122. For information on Louis Bedford's life, read *Quest For Justice*, by Darwin Payne. Govenar and Brakefield, *Deep Ellum*, 9-10.

phonetic spelling of "elm" by the Black and Jewish communities doing business in that area.[123] The two communities coexisted in that space, and the name "Deep Ellum" exists as the confluence of Black and Jewish cultures both suffering discrimination.

Early on, Deep Ellum was renowned for saloons, dance halls, gambling, liquor, and pawnshops. Bonnie and Clyde, the infamous mob couple, were even familiar faces in Deep Ellum during the 1930s.[124] There is an aptly named song, "Deep Elm Blues," originally recorded in 1933 by the Lone Star Cowboys for the Victor and Bluebird labels.[125] The song highlights the ways Deep Ellum held space for Dallas to cross boundaries.

As with any good folk song, there are variations from across the decades based on whomever happens to be singing, placing their own mark in the lyrics. The Shelton Brothers recorded an interpretation in 1935 describing a preacher who stopped preaching after he went down to Deep Ellum.[126] Deep Ellum is known for blues legends such as Blind Lemon Jefferson, Blind Willie Johnson, Alex Moore, Buster Smith, and Marvin Montgomery.

Deep Ellum continually proved to be a place where Black entrepreneurs and businesses thrived. The 1925 business directory lists everything from blacksmiths, landscapers, doctors, cafes, real estate agencies, tailors, dance schools, and ice dealers. The music and entertainment vibes in the area allowed for the development of Black cultural experiences drawing strong crowds week in and week out. The Black Elephant, the Swiss Airdrome Theater, Fat Jack's, the Star, the Mammoth, and the

123. Govenar and Brakefield, *Deep Ellum*, 5.
124. Ibid., 69.
125. Ibid., 19.
126. Ibid.

Park were just a few of the Black theaters in Deep Ellum. Theaters produced musical comedies, vaudeville, and blues shows, a musical legacy which continues even to the present day iteration of Deep Ellum, despite a change in demographics.[127]

For an area renowned for its entertainment and night life, the 1930s would prove to be a difficult time for the area due to the Great Depression. Discretionary spending on shopping and entertainment declined, leaving theaters and music halls in the position of moving or closing down. What began was a slow shift of Black community institutions to the North Dallas district just north up Central Track.[128]

Into the '40s, there still remained some remnants of that old Deep Ellum style. Music was still being played and street preachers were still attempting to convert street corners. The decade would also be heavily associated with violent crime in the area. Rather than referring to a hot lunch item, the "Deep Ellum Special" became a reference for long switchblade knives often used for stabbings in the area.[129]

Post-World War II, there was an effort by police to reform the Deep Ellum patrol beat. Violent crime was targeted heavily in the area, with Police Chief Carl Hansson informing officers to "not worry about complaints." Fifty years later, retired Officer Gus Edwards recalled in an interview with Alan Govenar how officers focused on the "pimps, hustlers and whores" since they discerned the majority of crimes could be tied back to them.[130]

———

127. Ibid., 49-53.
128. Ibid., 208.
129. "Deep Ellum Extra Special," *Dallas Morning News*, December 12, 1940.
130. Govenar and Brakefield, *Deep Ellum*, 215.

Narrative Foundations

Even as early as 1925, Dallas began developing narratives about Deep Ellum. The *Dallas Morning News*, in an article highlighting the "Hidden Gems of Dallas' Black Belt," reviewed the ways Black residents spent their time in "Darkytown."[131] Nestled within the overtly racist article is a prime example of how White definitions of neighborhood construction are considered the standard, and anything that deviates is written off as less than.

The author, William Ward, describes Deep Ellum as a place in the "gathering shadows" that puts White citizens on alert if they are to venture into Deep Ellum. Ward offhandedly describes Indiana Street, just a block north of the central Elm-Main-Commerce streets, as "[not being] dignified by such a title (street)…[and] is just the appendage of a real street." Descriptions of the "rows" and "alleys" play up Black life in Deep Ellum like a caricature from a Blackface novelty show because "the Negro race is in its childhood."[132]

Toward the end of the article, Ward describes some of the then newer Black neighborhood additions, usually a few blocks, in Dallas like Queen City in South Dallas and the Booker T. Washington addition in North Dallas. The White narrative of Black Dallas is very clear at this point:

"Hundreds of Negroes live in these sections. They have their own business establishments and apparently are happy. But the 'Negro additions' of Dallas do not represent the real Negro spirit. The old-time darky and the 'jazz-lovin' sheik',

---

131. William Ward, "Hidden Nooks of Dallas' Black Belt," *Dallas Morning News*, November 29, 1925.
132. Ibid.

who is a son of the ancient Negro, are the types that made the alleys and rows of Dallas famous."[133]

Ward goes out of his way to strip the dignity of the new additions and progress Black residents made in spite of restrictions on space, capital, access to decision-making, and political power. Even when Black spaces were built in a way mirroring traditional White neighborhoods, they were still viewed as less than because they were Black. This is how narratives perpetuate and devaluate.

Andre Perry of the Brookings Institute found significant correlations in the devaluation of neighborhoods as the proportion of Black homeowners increased. Holding all other metrics the same—like housing type, crime rates, schools, and access to businesses—the research found homes in majority Black neighborhoods were valued at 23 percent less than neighborhoods with few or no Black residents. The average loss in 2018 Black home values across the United States was $48,000 per home, or $156 billion in total.[134] Just to emphasize, Black homeowners in the United States are losing out on $156 billion in asset wealth.

For the sake of our purposes in this book, I would argue those losses are due in large part to the narratives perpetuated about Black spaces, starting before the 1925 *News* article and continuing into the present day. This prejudice stems from a deficit-based mentality where White is held as the standard by which we measure the value of things. Even in this book, while I may critique the White point of view, I still use Whiteness as the comparison rather than centering

---

133. Ibid.
134. Andre Perry, Jonathan Rothwell, and David Harshbarger, *The Devaluation of Assets in Black Neighborhoods: The Case of Residential Property* (Washington, DC: The Brookings Institution, 2018), 15.

BIPOC as an asset to be valued against.[135] Narrative changes begin with interrogating our own biases, the way we assign value, and how we perpetuate those biases and values in our everyday lives.

———

"Deep Ellum Is Doomed"

Ward's 1925 *News* article contained a subheading titled "Deep Ellum Doomed." The section implied the encroaching Dallas skyline was tightening its grip on this part of town and the skyline would soon be the downfall of Deep Ellum.[136]

Nearly one hundred years later, the Dallas skyline came close but never quite made it to Deep Ellum. The Great Depression showed up before anything else. A crunch on housing options for Black citizens of Dallas forced many Deep Ellum residents to cross the Trinity into predominantly white neighborhoods in South Dallas, eventually leading to bombings of Black homes.

That same decade, the H&TC railroad tracks, which originally proved a boon for the area in the late nineteenth and early twentieth century, were removed. The H&TC railroad ties along Central Track were pulled up in preparation for the development of Central Expressway. Like North Dallas, this once porous north-south border between Deep Ellum and downtown Dallas transformed into a more significant

---

135. For further discussion on this topic, see Chapter 8: Space, Place, and Justice.
136. William Ward, "Hidden Nooks of Dallas' Black Belt," *Dallas Morning News*, November 29, 1925.

and visible barrier literally and figuratively sealing off Deep Ellum from downtown Dallas.

"The part that disappeared [from Deep Ellum] was the culture of Central [Track], which was where all the Black businesses were located. And that was intentional, you know? It was not accidental," Govenar lamented to me.

Black businesses like the Gypsy Team Room were pulled up and removed like the ties of the railroad track, creating a void the new six-lane highway filled. Displaced citizens either followed others to South Dallas or pushed further north to the newly built Black neighborhood, Hamilton Park, which was designed to be far away from the city.[137]

As if the decades were attempting to deal Deep Ellum a knockout, the '50s exacerbated vehicle-related infrastructure woes. In a pattern similar to North Dallas and other neighborhoods, trains served as a boon for Black and Brown neighborhoods and, conversely, automobile infrastructure often served the desires of motorists outside the neighborhoods' infrastructure who passed through.

On the west end of Deep Ellum, Good-Latimer Expressway was completed as part of the Central Expressway network in 1956, helping traffic move into and back out of the eastern downtown district.[138] Good-Latimer further displaced Black businesses when Good Street was widened, accommodating extra lanes and creating additional north-south barriers between Deep Ellum and downtown Dallas.

For context, Good Street already rang as a symbol of White supremacy in the neighborhood. District Judge John Jay Good, former Confederate officer, secessionist, and mayor

---

137. Govenar and Brakefield, *Deep Ellum*, 215.
138. "Expressway Nears Completion," *Dallas Morning News*, July 12, 1956.

of Dallas, is described as "an impediment to reconstruction."[139] Good fought to keep Freedmen and Unionists off of juries and created conditions where those who murdered Unionists and Freemen were let off with a warning and given time to flee the county, free from facing justice.[140] Adding Latimer's name to the expressway elevated the pro-slavery newspaper editor's name into everyday use.[141]

Another element further encouraging traffic flow for Elm Street came through making it a one-way street and installing parking meters. In effect, traffic was forced west toward downtown and away from Deep Ellum. This was enough to cause protest by business owners on the street, who staged a march up Elm Street carrying a coffin to represent the death of the neighborhood.[142]

———

Small actions like traffic routing may seem trivial at first pass. I would argue this demonstration shows people are paying attention to even the smallest changes in the city around them. Something as small as traffic direction can have dramatic effects on people's lives and livelihoods. What may make sense on paper could have wider, unintended—or perhaps intended—consequences.

139. "John Jay Good," Texas State Historical Association Handbook of Texas, accessed February 27, 2021.

140. Unionists were understood to be White men loyal to the Union. Randolph B. Campbell, *Grass-Roots Reconstruction in Texas, 1865-1880* (Baton Rouge: Louisiana State University Press, 1997), 73-75.

141. Bruce Roche, "Latimer, James Wellington (1825-1859)," Texas State Historical Association Handbook of Texas, accessed February 27, 2021.

142. Govenar and Brakefield, *Deep Ellum*, 215.

One final blow came for Deep Ellum in the '60s, as Central Expressway was redesigned to be an elevated structure through Deep Ellum. This section of Central Expressway eventually became part of the Interstate Highway System and renamed I-345.

Elevating this portion of Central was in discussion at least as far back as 1954.[143] In the late '60s, the City began acquiring right-of-way and purchased two blocks of Elm Street perpendicular to the highway, razing buildings along the path. Residents were also shocked by the news in 1966 that this elevated highway would be next door and called it the "end of Deep Elm." The *DMN* agreed this highway construction would "cut the heart out of the district."[144] With an increase in through car traffic and a decrease in foot traffic, the lifeblood of any business district, residents and business owners knew this would be a huge blow to what was affectionately referred to as "The Street."[145]

Former Deep Ellum residents tended to point to several reasons for why Deep Ellum declined. Former resident Ernestine Claunch speculated "that the growth of strip shopping centers and then malls changed the shopping patterns of people who patronized small businesses. Moreover, integration and upward mobility for African Americans and Jews created new business and housing opportunities."[146] Eddie Goldstein, son of famous pawnbroker "Honest Joe" Goldstein, didn't "think Central Expressway killed Deep Ellum as much

143. Allen Quinn, "Four-Level Grade Separation Considered for Expressways," *Dallas Morning News*, June 20, 1954.
144. Kent Biffle, "Freeway to Cut Fabled Street," *Dallas Morning News*, June 26, 1966.
145. Ibid.
146. Govenar and Brakefield, *Deep Ellum*, 207.

as two things: television and integration."[147] I did not expect integration to pop up in my research as one of Deep Ellum's original killers. It felt ironic that lack of segregation could aid in the decline of a communal Black space.

Black families continued to migrate to South and West Dallas and Hamilton Park, leaving Deep Ellum behind. Businesses began shuttering in the 1950s. This precipitated a loss of small business revenue, as more options were available away from the downtown area; the development of strip malls also meant there were more diverse shopping opportunities available. In 1965, Dallas became home to the largest climate-controlled retail establishments in the world when Northpark Mall was built by Raymond Nasher just a few miles north of Deep Ellum. With the pieces of the community that had so strongly tied it together earlier in the century gone, Deep Ellum, as it was known, largely began to disintegrate.

———

The Nine (or Three) Lives of Deep Ellum

Over the years since the original roots of Deep Ellum were planted, the neighborhood has worked to find the balance between development and paying homage to its past.[148] My typical path through Deep Ellum takes me along Good-Latimer Expressway past the Pythian Temple, over Elm, Main, and Commerce streets, then underneath I-345. I pass

---

147. Ibid., 215.
148. *Deep Ellum Public Improvement District Strategic Plan* (Dallas: Deep Ellum Foundation, 2019): 2.

restaurants, bars, clubs, and the old Ford Model-T factory/ Adams Hat/Loft building, and other venues reminding passersby that history deserves a seat at the table in our lives today.

There are proposals to tear down I-345 as it nears the end of its safe operating life. Removal of the elevated highway that towers over the neighborhood and contributed to its demise could be a catalyst for knitting Deep Ellum back into the fabric of downtown Dallas. Coalition For a New Dallas estimates removal of the highway would make "245 acres largely defined by empty parking lots and undeveloped land into a mixed-use, mixed-income neighborhood that will generate jobs, create affordable housing, and improve the quality of life for all of Dallas' residents."[149]

Dallas Area Rapid Transit (DART) is in the process of designing a new rail line in downtown Dallas.

I am now haunted by the decisions I used to make about locating pipeline facilities. Making decisions about traffic flow on a street is not much different from gas or water flowing in a pipeline and building or taking a pipeline out of service is not much different from building or removing a highway.

Infrastructural decisions are often made to support high-growth areas or places considered important by municipal or utility officials. I noticed this most often when projects would move from lower-income and industrial areas toward higher-income areas. Designs that received less pushback and more autonomy from an engineering perspective in low-income areas were placed under greater scrutiny than those same designs in higher-income areas.

---

149. "I-345: Replace I-345 and Rebuild Dallas," Coalition for a New Dallas, accessed November 10, 2020.

Looking back, I realize the privilege afforded to me as a utility engineer to make small decisions because of my expertise. My knowledge and relative power had outsized influence in lower-income and industrial areas with less organized engagement. I continue to come back to the questions: Who makes the final decisions in this neighborhood? Who benefits from them?

Who is left out?

4

THE PARK LEFT STANDING

———

"[Little Mexico] was a wonderful place to play, visit family, and visit neighborhood stores. There was a little grocery store on almost every corner, or a tortillería on every corner, or a little restaurant or café," Sol Villasana remembers. For Albert González, "Little Mexico was like a big family."[150]

Now, the neighborhood is gone.

"In slow motion, one of this city's most significant neighborhoods—once, junkyards and dumping grounds salvaged by Jewish and Mexican immigrants who then could live nowhere else—has vanished. We noticed, yes, but could do nothing but watch, mourn and keep driving to work."[151] When I first read Robert Wilonsky's words in the *Dallas Morning News*, they hit me like a brick. I didn't catch the neighborhood in time.

———

150. Texas Historical Commission, "Dallas' Little Mexico," September 23, 2015, video, 2:28.
151. Robert Wilonsky, "Farewell to 'the Last Remnants' of Dallas' Little Mexico, as Houses on Harry Hines, Harwood Await Demolition," *Dallas Morning News*, December 13, 2019.

Whenever I talk about Little Mexico to people who live in Dallas, it's a similar refrain. Many people remember seeing these homes as they came into downtown. If you're from Dallas, you might remember the old white house with the craftsman windows and green roof on your left as you drove down Harry Hines, thinking to yourself, "Wow, these old houses look incredibly out of place," or, "Why do these vacant lots just have steps leading to nothing." Someone lived there—that was Charlie Villasana's house.

I've personally taken the Dallas North Tollway into downtown Dallas through the heart of the former neighborhood several times over the years. I noticed the out-of-place homes and businesses amongst the new towering skyscrapers. I might have paused to consider what used to be here; however, as Wilonsky notes, most of the time I simply drove by. Much like the Freedman's Cemetery in North Dallas, I was too concerned with whatever was going on in my life to stop and ask "why?"

Reading Wilonsky's words eight months after the destruction of the last houses in Little Mexico brought feelings of anger and sadness. It is a similar feeling I have had along much of this journey of writing and researching this book.

The last two remaining homes in Dallas' largest *barrio* (neighborhood), known as Little Mexico, were demolished in early 2020. A small plaque and a few buildings are the only remaining evidence of the former neighborhood amidst the tall skyscrapers, the American Airlines Center, and Victory Plaza.[152]

The century-old Pike Park is still there, home to quinceañeras, fiestas, and Mexican Independence Day celebrations for

---

152. The American Airlines Center is home of the Dallas Mavericks basketball and Dallas Stars hockey teams.

generations.[153] St. Ann's, a former Catholic school serving Little Mexico, was partially spared demolition through becoming a registered landmark in 1999, leaving it still standing ninety-three years later.[154] St. Ann's Commercial High School, serving young women in Little Mexico, was demolished. The remaining school building once serving boys in Little Mexico, was the first building in Dallas with a Mexican history to be declared a landmark and is now home to a restaurant and bar.[155] The Little Mexico Village apartments built in 1942, the first Mexican American public housing project in Dallas, stand out as brightly painted mission style adobe amidst the modern glass skyscrapers. Aside from those few structures, little physical evidence of Little Mexico remains.

Creation of Little Mexico

(Spoiler Alert: Railroads & Conflict Ahead)

Much like other areas of Dallas, railroad infrastructure played a starring role in the development of the Little Mexico community. In the 1880s, the Missouri, Kansas, and Texas (MKT) railroad came through Dallas slightly later than the Texas & Pacific (T&P) and the Houston and Texas Central (H&TC). The

---

153. Quinceañeras are a celebration of a girl's 15th birthday.
154. "Dallas Landmark Commission Landmark Nomination Form: St. Ann's School/St. Ann's Com. H. S. / Guadalupe Social Center," City of Dallas Neighborhood Designation Task Force, September 8, 1998.
155. "Home," St. Ann's Alumni & Friends of Little Mexico, Inc., accessed November 5, 2020.

MKT joined two rail lines together in Dallas, one coming north from Denton and the other coming east from Greenville.[156]

Mexican workers aided construction of the rail lines in the 1870s to 1880s and, much like Deep Ellum and North Dallas, a sparse community developed alongside the tracks. Workers first sought housing in abandoned railroad cars in the MKT rail yard in downtown, but not long after began settling north of downtown in an area already an enclave for poorer Eastern European Jewish immigrants.[157] Little Mexico was taking root.

Transportation was not the only factor shaping the development of Little Mexico; revolution brewed on the other side of the border at the turn of the century. For ten years, starting in 1910, a power struggle arose after the thirty-one-year-long regime of Mexico's president, Porfirio Díaz. The armed conflict led many families to seek refuge north of the border in Texas.

In 1910, there were just 583 Mexican immigrants in Dallas, which blossomed to 2,902 in 1920 and then tripled by 1930.[158] Around the same time, much of the working Jewish population began pushing south of the Trinity River into the Cedars and South Dallas neighborhoods, as they were part of the rising middle class and able to afford larger homes there for their families.[159]

Farming, cotton picking, and service work in downtown businesses and hotels provided the bulk of employment

---

156. The MKT railway is known today as the Katy Trail. "Route Maps," Katy Railroad Historical Society, accessed September 1, 2020.

157. Gwendolyn Rice, "Little Mexico and the Barrios of Dallas," in *Dallas Reconsidered: Essays in Local History*, ed. Michael V. Hazel (Dallas: Three Forks Press, 1995), 159.

158. Ibid., 158-9.

159. Elvia Limón, "What's the History behind the Little Mexico Village Apartments in Uptown? Curious Texas Investigates," *Dallas Morning News*, January 9, 2019.

opportunities in Little Mexico, while entrepreneurship proved to be a wide-reaching legacy for the community. The community, isolated from the remainder of the city due to Jim Crow laws, was forced to develop communal infrastructure on its own, and it did. Bakeries, beauty salons, movie theaters, photography studios, restaurants, and tortilla factories helped create a vibrant and textured life in Little Mexico.[160]

Maria Luna arrived in Dallas in 1923 from San Luis Potosi, Mexico, with her two children, Carmen and Francisco X, unable to speak English. While working at a grocery store, Maria purchased a repossessed corn grinder and put her business skills learned from running a butcher shop in Mexico to the test. Luna's Tortilla Factory opened in 1924, less than a year after Maria arrived in Dallas.[161]

As her business grew, Maria needed additional employees who knew how to make tortillas, and skeptical husbands did not want their wives working outside of the home. Maria bypassed this by delivering masa to women in the morning and picking up tortillas later that day.[162] Eventually, Maria hired twenty-five women to work inside the factory, initially producing five hundred tortillas a day.[163] Luna's tortilla customers expanded to other barrios in the area: New Orleans, Oklahoma, and as far as St. Louis, even becoming one of the original ingredients for making Frito's.[164] Maria's entrepreneurial spirit is representative of the Mexican-American community in Dallas.

160. Sol Villasana, *Dallas's Little Mexico* (Charleston: Arcadia Publishing, 2011), 77.
161. "Dallas Landmark Commission Landmark Nomination Form: Luna Tortilla Factory," ibid.
162. Masa is ground corn used to make tortillas.
163. A. C. Greene, "Woman's Determination Shaped Tortilla Factory," *Dallas Morning News*, July 7, 1991.
164. "Dallas Landmark Form: Luna Tortilla Factory," ibid.

While Little Mexico had a thriving business sector, substandard housing was a significant concern as in other segregated areas outside downtown Dallas (e.g., North Dallas, etc.). A 1935 "Blighted Area Survey of Dallas, Texas" showed 40 percent of the homes in Little Mexico being considered "unfit for occupancy" and only 2 percent in "good condition." Dallas's same Jim Crow segregation laws creating overcrowding conditions in North Dallas also influenced conditions in Little Mexico. The survey found 74 percent of the homes in Little Mexico to be overcrowded.[165]

When the Dallas Housing Authority (DHA) decided to move forward with public housing for Little Mexico in the early 1940s, only eight dwellings needed to be cleared for the fourteen-acre site.[166] Opening in September 1942, just months after Roseland Homes, 102 additional units of housing became available to the community, providing some relief to the overcrowded conditions.

Turney Street

FDR's New Deal gave birth to the Federal Works Progress Administration (WPA) on May 6, 1935, with an appropriation just shy of $5 billion.[167] Dealy Plaza, where President Kennedy

---

165. Gwendolyn Rice, ibid., 162.
166. Robert B. Fairbanks, *The War on Slums in the Southwest: Public Housing and Slum Clearance in Texas, Arizona, and New Mexico, 1935-1965* (Philadelphia: Temple University Press, 2014), 65.
167. Jason Scott Smith, *Building New Deal Liberalism: The Political Economy of Public Works, 1933-1956* (New York: Cambridge University Press, 2006), 87.

would years later be assassinated, was one of the larger WPA projects in Dallas.

In Little Mexico, the WPA directed a quarter of a million dollars in funding toward paving and widening Turney Street in order to ease congestion coming into and out of the north side of Dallas.[168] Turney ran parallel to the MKT railroad and was identified as a potential connection to the Denton Highway heading north out of downtown. Members of the community donated small strips of property for the widening in exchange for not having to pay for curb, gutter, and sidewalk improvements. Based on *DMN* reports, other property in Little Mexico appears to have gone through a controversial assessment and condemnation process.[169] Without adequate primary records at the time of writing, I could see this being consistent with other projects in minority neighborhoods in Dallas. It would be a specter of future predatory development practices.

Residents of Little Mexico felt widening Turney Street would create a north-south barrier through their community, isolating one side of Little Mexico from the other. For the rest of Dallas, the project was seen as the beginning of exploration into an otherwise unknown neighborhood that "quite likely [would] come in for a little development."[170] It is presumed that this development would be different from what existed in Little Mexico at the time, likely new and White.

A *DMN* writer describes the nature of Little Mexico in 1940 as an oddity within the broader context of the developed and improved city, because it was largely considered

---

168. "Officials Jubilant at Approval Given Highway Projects," *Dallas Morning News*, October 2, 1937.

169. "Council Gets Tracts for Turney Route," *Dallas Morning News*, July 27, 1939.

170. "Turney Street Connection," *Dallas Morning News*, February 15, 1940.

undeveloped in the eyes of White Dallas. Like a new land, the Turney street project paved the way for unexplored Little Mexico to be "opened up" and improved.[171]

I find this description of Little Mexico in relation to Dallas and the Turney Street project to be a key insight into how under-resourced neighborhoods are often seen as blank canvases for redevelopment as soon as a little investment starts trickling in. The implication is the area had no value before the road came through, and only after the infrastructure was in place did Little Mexico become an asset to the greater Dallas community. I've asked myself the following questions many times: Why was Little Mexico "an oddity" to begin with? What does this say about how we view our neighbors? How do we see their agency in shaping their own communities? Who determines the value of space?

A year after completion of the widening, Turney Street was renamed Harry Hines Boulevard, honoring the former Texas highway commissioner and signaling change in the neighborhood.[172]

Tollway Casualties

In 1959, the decision was made to build the Dallas North Tollway along the route of the old St. Louis Southwestern "Cotton Belt" railroad route running north out of downtown.[173]

171. Ibid.
172. "Ribbon Road Barrier Snipped," *Dallas Morning News*, October 15, 1941.
173. Oscar Slotboom, *Dallas-Fort Worth Freeways: Texas-Sized Ambition* (Totowa, NJ: Lightning Press, 2014), 229.

As was common practice for Dallas highways, railroad right-of-way would be converted to highway use. The new tollway was designed to transport residents from wealthy White Dallas suburbs directly into northern downtown Dallas via Harry Hines.

Eminent domain was the land acquisition tool utilized for connecting the Tollway to Harry Hines. Little Mexico homeowners were forced to sell their homes for an average price of $10,000, which at the time was arguably not enough to cover relocation expenses.[174] Remaining residents in Little Mexico were forced to contend with the precarious position of a neighborhood divided by a heavily trafficked six-lane-wide street no longer easily crossed. Charlie Villasana, a Little Mexico resident and grocery store owner, later recalled, "When I saw that toll road getting built, I said, 'Oh hell, this is going to be murder for us.'"[175]

As we've seen in several instances, highways and roads can alter the living patterns for those living in the community while primarily serving interests on the outside.

Sol Villasana, Charlie's cousin, also grew up in Little Mexico and experienced Dallas's highway building boom and remembers Saturday barbecue runs he and his father used to take. He recalls, "I had to have been six, seven, or eight... we would just go downtown, [and] cross right over" into South Dallas. When I-30 was constructed on the south side of downtown, the highway created a gulf right before his eyes. No longer were they able to simply move through downtown—they had to contend with the "monstrous gash" left by the construction, literally chopping South Dallas

174. Rice, ibid., 165.
175. Cassandra Jaramillo, "Dallas' Little Mexico Is Nearly Gone in Uptown, but Here's What Remains," *Dallas Morning News*, March 14, 2018.

neighborhoods in half. It comes by the nickname "The Canyon" honestly.

From that experience, Sol began to grasp the devastation this and other highway construction could cause. Even something as simple as going to get barbecue was becoming an artifact of the past for him. The restaurant was "perched on the edge of where they cut the south side," and if you went too close you would "sort of fall off into the canyon." Losing that small tradition with his father opened up his "kid's mind, [and he] began to realize that there would be casualties."

His words caught me off guard. While I have grown to understand the ways we lose our history when we engage in demolition or infrastructure development, I had not considered it as a casualty until then.

With the tollway cutting through the neighborhood, it became more difficult to access Pike Park on the west side of Little Mexico, eventually leading to declined use.[176] Land acquisition for Woodall Rodgers in the 1970s decimated the southern edge of Little Mexico, where the Klyde Warren Deck Park stands today.[177] The Luna Tortilla Factory (now Meso Maya) and El Fenix Mexican Restaurant, once part of the fabric of Little Mexico, now face a wall of concrete as the underground expressway raises up and overhead, asserting its presence.

---

176. David Preziosi, "Lost + Found: Pike Park—Little Mexico's Struggle for its Oasis," *Columns Magazine*, Winter 2020.

177. Darwin Payne, *Big D: Triumphs and Troubles of an American Supercity in the 20th Century* (Dallas: Three Forks Press, 1994), 344.

Zoning and Xonsequences

"Spot zoning" increased in the '6os, further deteriorating the community.[178]

In most Little Mexico cases, land would be zoned for residential, multi-family uses one would expect for a neighborhood (homes, duplexes, small stores, etc.). Developers began purchasing individual lots and applying to the City for a change in zoning, usually to commercial purposes, leading to a loss of the neighborhood fabric. The *Dallas Morning News* reported "the problem is that with development on all sides, the area [became] a residential pocket, headed toward a transition that [would] be unpleasant for property owners who [chose]... to remain."[179] The commercial development was not designed to support the neighborhood—think less suburb shopping center, more high-rise office buildings.

In 1970, Little Mexico resident Gus Calderone indicated Little Mexico residents were aware when "the Tollway was coming in... it would create these problems. For the last ten years, there's been one rezoning case after another."[180] Sol Villasana described how the development was fundamentally a problem of representation: "The fact that there were older people [who might be] more susceptible to land grabs

---

178. Spot zoning refers to the practice of purchasing a property and applying for a change in the land use (zoning). Zoning is the method cities use to determine how land can be used and is generally used as a protective measure, preventing disparate uses from being next to each other. For example, you wouldn't want to put a garbage incinerator (industrial) next to a single family home (residential) because that could cause adverse health effects for residents living next door.

179. Carolyn Barta, "Residential Pocket Faces Uncertain Future," *Dallas Morning News,* May 24, 1970.

180. Ibid.

(by developers), there was nobody representing them personally, legally, and nobody representing at City Hall. That had a lot to do with the ease by which developers [could purchase land]."

What was left of the tight knit community was quickly being plucked up by developers and other parties from outside the community. Some Little Mexico residents were open to selling. Calderone said residents wanted to "block up the land and sell it to a development. But spot zoning [was] hampering this."[181] Selling the land as a unified block benefitted the neighborhood's interests because they would all leave in unison, rather than slowly, one by one. It's the difference between leaving a party together with your friends or watching your friends slowly leave a party until you're left alone by yourself.

The City Council was responsible for approving zoning changes; sometimes this went against the wishes of not only the neighborhood but also the City Plan Commission. Without representation on City Council to advocate for their voices, it was difficult for Little Mexico's residents to block spot zoning practices. Either way, City Planning Director James Schroeder did not have a strong outlook for the future of the community, given the "higher intensity use" surrounding the neighborhood.[182]

When Albert González, co-founder of the Dallas Mexican American Historical League (DMAHL) in 2008, spoke with me about this time, he recalled, "[we] were ignored." The neighborhood was clearly changing, and it became clearer that the changes were not meant to include existing

181. Ibid.
182. Ibid.

Little Mexico residents. Albert's grandmother, who did not speak English, had difficulty navigating the neighborhood. González said they advocated on her generation's behalf saying, "If you're going to start putting in traffic lights and all that in there, put them also in Spanish."

Pike Park at the Center

In 1911, when the world around Little Jerusalem was shifting from residential to industrial, the Kessler Plan suggested the City of Dallas purchase land on the northwestern side of downtown for a new park to serve the neighborhood children.[183] In 1913, the Turney and White families sold nearly four and a half acres of land to the City for development of Summit Play Park.[184] A year later, the two-story Spanish revival community center was finished, and the park opened to the public. The two-story building commanded a large presence atop the chalky white hill the park is situated on.

As one of the few places Mexican Americans could congregate in segregated Dallas, Pike Park quickly became the center of Mexican-American life in the neighborhood and was the place of choice for large celebrations. These were the only conditions under which Mexican Americans were allowed to use the park initially. Prior to 1931, the park was not labeled for Mexican American use until the Dallas Park

---

183. "Dallas Landmark Structures and Sites: Pike Park," City of Dallas Office of Historic Preservation, accessed November 10, 2020. David Preziosi, "Lost + Found," *Columns*, Winter 2020.

184. Villasana, *Dallas's Little Mexico*, 14.

Board designated Pike Park for joint use that year. All other parks remained "Whites Only."[185]

Pancho Medrano, Little Mexico resident and activist, remembered, "There was a swimming pool there and we could not use the swimming pool… or the swings, or any of the park, we were not allowed inside the park."[186] He recalled not being able to watch summer movies, as "the park patrol would whistle at us and tell us to get away."[187] In 1938, after several years of working with the Mexican Consul, Mexican-American children were allowed to swim in the pool from 7 a.m. to 9 a.m.[188] Even as Mexican-American kids were allowed to swim in the pool, Pancho recalled, "It was cold… in the dirty water that was left over from the day before when the [White] kids swam there."[189]

The thought of even indirect contact (swimming in the same water) with Mexicans led to extreme measures upon Mexican-American children using the pool.[190] Pancho remembered the routine injustice, saying,

> "At fifteen minutes before nine, they would tell us to get out of the pool…[Parks Employees] would empty out the water from the pool and make us clean the pool before putting in new water for the White kids who would use the pool the rest of the day. They would also make us pick up trash in the park and check us

185. *KERA*, "Little Mexico: El Barrio (1997)," August 1, 2013, video, 28:57.
186. Ibid.
187. Carol Trujillo, "Dallas' First Barrio," *Dallas Morning News*, September 13, 1987.
188. Michael Phillips, *White Metropolis: Race, Ethnicity, and Religion in Dallas, 1841-2001* (Austin: University of Texas Press, 2006), 70.
189. *KERA*, "Little Mexico: El Barrio (1997)."
190. Michael Phillips, *White Metropolis*, 70.

real closely for body sores and lice. Then, while we were cleaning, the White kids would call us the usual names, 'wetbacks' and that kind of thing, and even pee in the water that we would use the next day."[191]

As the Jewish community began moving to larger homes in South Dallas, the Mexican-American community started referring to Pike Park as "our park."[192] It has served as home of quinceañeras, Cinco de Mayo, and Mexican Independence day celebrations for generations of Mexican Americans in Dallas.[193]

While Pike Park has a long history of celebration within the community, it also fought for its life at least three times in the course of its nearly 110-year history:

1. In the early 1950s, the City sought to close the park until the community fought back in support of it remaining open. At the end of the following decade, in 1969, the construction of the Dallas North Tollway began to have a physical and psychological impact on Little Mexico. With the highway cutting through the neighborhood, it was more difficult to access the park and use began to decline.[194]

2. In 1969, Anita Martinez, the first Mexican-American to serve on Dallas's City Council (and in the United States), fought the second attempt to close the park.[195]

191. Roy H. Williams and Kevin J. Shay, *Time Change: An Alternative View of the History of Dallas* (Dallas: To Be Publishing Co., 1991), 64.

192. David Preziosi, "Lost + Found" *Columns,* Winter 2020.

193. Geoff Montes, "Preserving Latino History at Pike Park in Dallas," National Trust for Historic Preservation, December 22, 2014.

194. David Preziosi, ibid.

195. Amy Simpson, *Pike Park: The Heart and History of Mexican Culture in Dallas* (Dallas: Los Barrios Unidos Community Clinic, 1981), 9.

She called Pike Park "the psychological heart of the Mexican American community in Dallas" and rallied the community and Council support to keep it open.[196]

3. When Santos Rodriguez, a twelve-year-old boy, was murdered by Dallas Police Officer Darrell Cain in 1973, the community turned to Pike Park.[197] It became the rallying point for protests and vigils, and the recreation center now bears his name. In the heart of the economic recession of the '80s, the City sought to get rid of the eighty-four-thousand-dollar line item in its annual budget for Pike Park. Arguing for residents to use nearby Reverchon Park proved unsuccessful as the dwindling Little Mexico community fought for the final time to save the heart of their community.[198]

Albert Valtierra, president of DMAHL, remembers how Pike Park was still a vibrant part of the community into the 1980s. His employer, "Southwestern Bell, now AT&T, had an employee group somewhat similar to DMAHL and they were having fiestas [at Pike Park]... anywhere from five to ten thousand [people]... media was covering events there." Then things began to slow down.

"... little by little, as the neighborhood, just continued to be decimated. I think 'gentrified' is the kind word, you know—it just started going by the wayside. I'm sad about where [Pike Park] is," Valtierra lamented to me. A once thriving cultural center was left empty and decaying with no community to fill it. Residents were displaced by decades of

---

196. David Preziosi, ibid.
197. Robert Finklea, "Officer Suspended, Charged," *Dallas Morning News*, July 25, 1973.
198. David Preziosi, ibid.

infrastructure development and predatory zoning practices left nearly unchecked by Dallas political and business powers.

I want to make a critical distinction here. Neighborhood change, or turnover, is a common occurrence. Neighborhoods naturally change and develop over time. Imagine a street where over time the street stays the same but neighbors come and go over many years, leading to a different neighborhood than what existed originally. Neighborhood change does occur on those terms, and I see that change on the street I grew up on.

Of the thirty-one homes on our street, I estimate over 80 percent are occupied by different owners than in the 1990s. The neighborhood block I live on is completely different than the one I grew up on. However, the neighborhood looks relatively the same as it did twenty years ago.

An equitable distinction lies in the why and how neighborhood change takes place. For Little Mexico, the neighborhood was changed by stakeholders with outside interests and altered in a negative way for its residents. As the interview with Gus Calderon indicated in 1970, residents were not opposed to the neighborhood property being sold, but wanted it done with their input. Instead, they were bought out one by one, holding on to the remains of Little Mexico as long as they could.

―――――

Saving Pike Park

"Personally, I've taken my grandkids and we walk… what used to be Little Mexico, and I point out everything that used to be there," Albert González told me when we spoke on the phone in 2020. "I took them to the apartment at 1807 Avila Plaza where I grew up in the Little Mexico apartments, and we walked over to Pike Park. I took them to see where St. Ann's High School used to be, where Santos Rodriguez lived and over to where he was shot… where his grandparents lived, different places."

González remembers, "Pike Park is… where I learned how to play football, basketball, you know, honestly, that's where I met my wife. It was a neighborhood thing… Unfortunately, kids nowadays don't really know. No one ever experienced that."

The turn of the century saved Pike Park from becoming another one of Little Mexico's losses when it gained Dallas landmark status in 2000.[199] Over the years, the park has seen many changes. The second story of the community center was removed in the 1950s and the original pool was filled in and covered with a brick plaza and a bandstand. Other resident designed upgrades in 1978, and general restorations in 2013 restored the park and recreation center after one hundred years of service.[200]

In the shadows of the American Airlines Center, Pike Park serves as a reminder of the heart of Mexican-American space and culture in Dallas. The park neighbors a new little league baseball field built by Dallas Mavericks owner and *Shark Tank* investor Mark Cuban. A small playground, blue basketball court, the community center, and gazebo make up the majority of what remains in the park, and aside from the

199. "Dallas Landmark Structures and Sites: Pike Park," ibid.
200. "Community House Gets Repairs in Pike Park," *Dallas Morning News*, January 15, 1950. Henry Tatum, "Park's Identity Returned," *Dallas Morning News*, November 13, 1978.

juxtaposed Spanish Revival building and the intricate gazebo modeled after one in Monterrey, Mexico, there would be little evidence Pike Park served as the heart of Mexican American culture in Dallas. If you drive too quickly on Harry Hines you can easily drive right past it, getting lost in the maze of high-rise construction zones.

DMAHL is seeking for the City of Dallas to restore the community center and have it return to public service. Albert Valtierra hopes the building can continue to serve the Mexican-American and broader Dallas community by housing DMAHL's operations and host exhibits for the public. His talks with new Pike Park neighbors like the American Airlines Center and the Dallas Mavericks indicate there is an appetite for this kind of historical community collaboration. I, for one, hope recognition of the park and building's service to the community will continue to inspire voices to rise up in support of keeping the heart beating.

Robert Wilonsky's interview with Sol Villasana ended with a quote summarizing many of the same feelings I've had along this journey:

> "I talk to several people who don't remember Little Mexico," Villasana said. "It never existed in their sphere, and without help from the new property owners, it will all be lost. We need to be a little more aggressive as citizens to make sure these travesties don't happen, and that when there's redevelopment in historic areas, it keeps those memories alive. When history disappears, there's nothing left to fight for."[201]

---

201. Robert Wilonsky, ibid.

5

A NEIGHBORHOOD
DISAPPEARING ACT

———

"Tenth Street is Bleeding."[202]

This article headline caught my attention. I had recently learned about the Tenth Street neighborhood while researching the North Dallas Freedman's Town. I learned that North Dallas was far from the only Freedman's Town in Dallas and Tenth Street was one of the most complete Freedman's Towns left in the country. The imagery of a neighborhood bleeding highlighted the almost imperceptible disruption a cut can have from the outside in, and the steady outflow of life such a small incision can create.

When it comes to cuts, I know they almost always feel less drastic if I'm not the one experiencing the pain. I think to myself, "That's unfortunate, but it looks like it should heal." In the words of Monty Python, "It's just a flesh wound."[203] It's

---

202. Joanna Hampton and Robert Swann, "Tenth Street is Bleeding," *Columns*, Winter 2020.

203. Terry Gilliam and Terry Jones, *Monty Python and the Holy Grail* (Python (Monty) Pictures, 1975), DVD, 1:32:00.

an arm's length empathy, and I move on with my life.

For the person experiencing the cut, it's a completely different feeling; the initial shock of the cut creates a wince of pain and the flowing blood brings additional concern. How did this happen? Did it go through the skin? How do I clean this up? Is this life threatening? Will this become infected? How do I bandage this up and stop the bleeding? These and other questions race through our minds when we bleed. Surrounded by the proper resources or first aid kits, responding to a cut is a simple act carried out with very little thought: clean the wound, apply some antibiotic ointment, and cover with a bandage. Simple.

What if you find yourself bleeding with no access to bandages or other first aid supplies? Personally, I panic, frantically searching for anything to cover the cut and stop the bleeding. When I am finally able to MacGyver a bandage together, it tends to be more aptly described as "creative" than as "simple." More effort is required to achieve a non-bleeding state where a bandage can be found and applied and proper healing can take place. As the article title suggested, a neighborhood like Tenth Street might know a thing or two about this feeling.

———

Beginnings

Buried in 1844, two-month-old Martha Ann Wright has the oldest marked grave in Oak Cliff Cemetery. She is thought to be the third non-American-Indian child born in Dallas County. Two years after her burial, William S. Beaty, a Kentucky immigrant, deeded approximately ten acres out of his 640-acre tract west of the Trinity River for the cemetery. He wished for the plot to serve as a place where "the buried remains of [his] beloved brother may not be disturbed nor the land in which he lies be ploughed." I clearly need to step up my game in caring for my siblings.[204]

Beaty's settlement, originally known as Hord's Ridge, was platted as the Whites-only Oak Cliff in 1887.[205] Miller's Four Acres' subdivision planted the seed of Tenth Street freedmen's town just east of present day I-35 and south of Eighth Street: the current northern boundary of Oak Cliff Cemetery.[206] These particular four acres were outside Oak Cliff town limits and the Hord Survey area, meaning it was available for purchase by newly freed Black slaves.[207] It has been described as "a plot of land on the eastern edge of Oak Cliff accessed by a street with no name."

The Boswell family, Anthony and Hillary Andrew, made their way to the area in 1888 and began buying property and building homes.[208] Today, the corner of Anthony and Boswell Streets just north of Tenth Street give a nod to this history.[209] The Boswells and other formerly enslaved families joined them, constructing everything that a segregated Freedman neighborhood needed. Extending south from Eight Street toward the Cedar Creek Branch, the neighborhood contained two churches, grocery stores, a school, and dozens of homes.

The national economic panic of 1893, caused by the bursting of silver and railroad bubbles, led to bank and business

204. "History," Oak Cliff Cemetery, accessed December 23, 2020.
205. Ibid.
206. Rachel Stone, "Architecture at Risk: Six Endangered Oak Cliff Places," Advocate Oak Cliff, accessed December 23, 2020.
207. Hampton and Swann, "Tenth Street is Bleeding," *Columns*.
208. Stone, ibid.
209. Jennifer Rangel, "Dallas Must Focus on Preserving the Tenth Street Historic District," North Dallas Gazette, June 19, 2019.

failures across the United States, with many of the bank failures occurring in the south and west.[210] The panic did not spare Dallas and Oak Cliff. Desperate investors began selling lots to African Americans just to try and stay afloat, leading to an expansion of the Tenth Street neighborhood to the west. By 1900, Tenth Street was home to just over five hundred residents.[211]

Through the early part of the twentieth century, Tenth Street continued to thrive with businesses and other Black neighborhoods flanking it. To the north was The Bottom neighborhood, lying in the western banks of the Trinity River.[212] To the south and east of Cedar Creek and the Gulf, Colorado, and Santa Fe Railroad was The Heights neighborhood.[213] Former resident David Perry described the three neighborhoods as "[making] up the Black community in Oak Cliff."[214] Clarence Holoman, a lifetime Tenth Street resident, described the neighborhood as "the Mecca for Black people in [Dallas]," where "everybody knew everybody, and as a kid, if you did something, five minutes later the parents knew about it."[215]

Tenth Street had all of the amenities a community needed. A two-story commercial building was built in the heart of the neighborhood in 1925, the home to Wabash Drug Store and

210. "Texas Homestead Law and the Economic Depression of the 1890s," The History Engine, accessed December 23, 2020.

211. U.S. National Park Service, "National Register of Historic Places Registration Form: Tenth Street Historic District," June 17, 1994.

212. Bcworkshop, *Neighborhood Stories: Tenth Street* (Dallas, TX: Bcworkshop, 2013), 42-43.

213. Ibid.

214. *Buildingcommunityworkshop*, "Neighborhood Stories: Tenth Street," June 15, 2013, video, 27:42.

215. Ibid.

two other tenants remains standing today at the intersection of Tenth and Clif Streets.[216]

Melvin and Lobie Sims moved to Tenth Street from Wortham, Texas, in the 1920s. The Sims opened a dry cleaner in the 1940s, servicing Tenth Street and other Black neighborhoods in Dallas. Lou Nell Sims, Melvin and Lobie's granddaughter, recalled that her father Noble Sims "was the tailor, he knew how to make suits, shirts, he did a lot of alterations [in the community and] for some of the Black doctors that had offices in [Fair Park] like Dr. Flowers and Dr. Conrad."

Patricia Cox's family moved from Rosebud, Texas, to Tenth Street not long after the Sims. Aside from the numerous businesses, she remembers the smells of Tenth Street from her childhood. On Eighth Street there was a movie theater: "It was two-story with a little hotel on top... and the laundromat, and a store, and a barbecue place. Man, you could smell that barbecue and you knew just when he was done cooking it."

Sam C. Black, his wife Belle, and their family also had a profound influence on the business life in Tenth Street and Black Dallas as a whole. The Black family ran several successful businesses including "a domino parlor, a grocery store, a drugstore, a transfer company, and the Live and Let Live Barber Shop."[217] Samuel C. Black started the first Black funeral home in Dallas on Tenth Street in 1914.[218] Current Chief Executive Officer of Black & Clark Linda Marshall indicates, "Black residents in Dallas were not being buried by White funeral homes due to Jim Crow laws."[219]

---

216. U.S. National Park Service, "Tenth Street Historic District," June 17, 1994.
217. Hampton and Swann, ibid.
218. "Our History," Black & Clark Funeral Home, accessed December 23, 2020.
219. Ibid.

I've come to learn from residents that Tenth Street was about family, whether that meant the neighbors, the businesses, the buildings, or the streets. In the words of Ms. Cox, "it was just a self-sustaining neighborhood."

The Fraying of Tenth Street

The fabric of Tenth Street began to fray when Clarendon Drive was being improved and extended through the neighborhood in the 1940s.

E. A. Wood, a City of Dallas engineer at the time, began speaking about plans to extend Clarendon as the final phase of the overall Clarendon project connecting Dallas through Oak Cliff. Residents living south of downtown were looking for an increased number of ways to cross the Trinity River.[220] The 1945 Bartholomew City Plan called out Clarendon as one of the streets needed to complete the connection from the Corinth Street Viaduct crossing the Trinity and traveling west to Beckley Avenue (which is roughly where I-35 crosses today).[221]

As Clarendon cut through Tenth Street, it cut off the southeast corner of the original Miller's Four Acres, stranding it on the south side of the road.[222] Separating the neigh-

---

220. Bcworkshop, *Neighborhood Stories: Tenth Street*, 20.
221. City Plan Commission, *An Outline of the Master Plan* (Dallas, TX: City of Dallas City Plan Commission, 1946): 79. "Clarendon to Become Major Traffic Artery," *Dallas Morning News*, April 25, 1940.
222. Bcworkshop, *Neighborhood Stories: Tenth Street*, 46.

borhood would prove to have long-term consequences for the homes on the south side.[223]

Clarendon also capped off the Cedar Creek Branch flowing between Tenth Street and Betterton Circle to the south, demolishing thirty-six structures along it.[224] Patricia Cox remembers when the water ran behind her family home on Betterton Circle, "in the summer it was nice and cool to your feet, [and] we'd go down there and put our feet in there…" Not only was the creek lost, but David Perry also described how informal patterns were destroyed through the paving:

> "Before Clarendon, the area coming into the existing Betterton Circle area, there were foot beaten trails that had those communities walking back and forth between those communities. When Clarendon came in, it separated those communities."[225]

Ironically, driving along Clarendon today from the Trinity River to the Dallas Zoo, you will see new pathways worn along the sides of the road. Very few sidewalks exist along Clarendon, except where sparse new development added them over the years—other streets coming off of Clarendon don't have any sidewalks at all.

The widening of the Trinity River and the levee construction completed in 1932 created significant anticipation for the possibility of future development. Due to the onset of the Great Depression, the newly available land wasn't able to be sold and largely sat vacant through World War II and

---

223. When the rest of the neighborhood received historical designation, this side was left out.

224. Bcworkshop, *Neighborhood Stories: Tenth Street*, 46.

225. *Buildingcommunityworkshop*, "Neighborhood Stories: Tenth Street."

into the 1950s.[226] Leslie A. Stemmons led the effort to build the Trinity River Levees and died before the land would ever be developed. The vacant land along the Trinity River left a wide-open path suitable for the alignment and construction of I-35E.

Although Leslie passed away in 1939, the Stemmons family donated 102 acres of land west of downtown to help expedite construction of the freeway through Dallas.[227] The interstate was subsequently named after Stemmons. The land donation ushered the I-35E alignment toward a Trinity crossing just north of the Cadiz Street viaduct and into the north side of Oak Cliff, into the Bottom and Tenth Street neighborhoods. Tenth Street resident Patricia Cox said "[it] was basically what killed the area, when the freeway came through."[228]

Clarence Holoman remembers "all of the streets [in the neighborhood] used to run right through, Eighth, Ninth, Tenth."[229] The freeway cut south through the western portion of the neighborhood, just east of Jefferson Avenue.

David Perry recalled, "I-35 literally stripped the neighborhood, and cordoned it off... it came right down and busted... the area [the neighborhood] relied on."[230]

Four hundred sixty-six buildings and twelve blocks of Fleming Avenue were purchased and demolished through eminent domain during the construction.[231] Businesses like the Sims' cleaners were forced to move elsewhere in the

---

226. Oscar Slotboom, *Dallas-Fort Worth Freeways: Texas-Sized Ambition* (Totowa, NJ: Lightning Press, 2014), 182.

227. Ibid., 186.

228. *Buildingcommunityworkshop*, "Neighborhood Stories: Tenth Street."

229. Ibid.

230. Ibid.

231. Bcworkshop, *Neighborhood Stories: Tenth Street*, 47.

neighborhood, while others closed up shop. Like the path of a tornado, I-35E clear cut a strip the size of a football field through the neighborhood. The Black Bottom, Tenth Street, and Heights neighborhoods were physically separated from the predominantly White neighborhoods in Oak Cliff west of the highway. The City had officially designated it a "negro only" area just a decade before.[232]

Alterations to Tenth Street

Tenth Street's physical fabric was altered as well as its familial structure. With the construction of the highway, many families moved out of the neighborhood and the state. Noble Sims recalled families "began to leave to California, [and] Oklahoma." As desegregation occurred throughout the 1950s and 1960s, larger and newer housing options began to open up across the city and families left the neighborhood.[233]

"It wasn't that it was bad in this area—they wanted better housing, they wanted their children to branch out and see other parks and other schools," Clarence Holoman recalled. He said, "the die hards (like the Sims and Cox's) stayed, said 'we aren't giving this up.'"[234]

In the '40s, Tenth Street was zoned for duplex and single-family residential use, meaning it was a true "neighborhood area." Two decades later, the neighborhood zoning

232. Bethany Erickson, "Positive News, for Once, in Tenth Street Historic District," Candy's Dirt, May 30, 2019.
233. *Buildingcommunityworkshop*, "Neighborhood Stories: Tenth Street."
234. Ibid.

changed, and the homes were no considered "nonconform-ing." Unfortunately for Tenth Street, this meant all of the homes in the area were no longer considered "conforming" to the land use, which is a precarious existence if homes fall into disrepair.[235]

It's easiest to think of nonconforming uses as a structure built in accordance with the laws and policies of the time, but under new laws and policies, it no longer fits in. Non-conforming structures are generally allowed to stay standing because they were built properly at the time. Things get tricky when say a home is in need of repair or improvement and the zoning laws do not allow a nonconforming building to be built up again. In short, during this time, a Tenth Street home needing significant repair could potentially not be repaired, forcing the land and structure to comply with current zoning regulations, which at the time were not residential.[236]

New City of Dallas zoning policies in 1984 set out to pro-tect and stabilize residential neighborhoods in the city. Tenth Street did not return to a residentially zoned area. Instead, the neighborhood was named a "future growth corridor" where commercial, retail, industrial manufacturing, and townhomes were allowed uses.[237] The City continued to view the neighborhood differently than residents did. Around this same time, Patricia Cox remembers "[the City of Dallas] used to wash the streets once a month, and they would sweep it with a street sweeper, and they stopped that." Residents experienced these changes as an attempt by the City to begin taking over the neighborhood for development.

---

235. Erickson, ibid.
236. "Non-Conforming Users," Pace University Elisabeth Haub School of Law, accessed December 26, 2020.
237. Erickson, ibid.

The three to four decades following the construction of I-35 saw population and housing stock decline in the Tenth Street neighborhood, very similar to North Dallas. Residents continued to leave and housing stock diminished. By the early '90s, a third of the lots in The Bottom, Tenth Street, and Heights areas were vacant, and 583 buildings in those neighborhoods were demolished between 1979 and 1995.[238]

Wait, Isn't This History?

Historic districts could be considered a way to preserve and protect history—places and spaces where history is neatly packaged and give a glimpse into history of time gone by. That is often not enough to save some neighborhoods from erasure; Tenth Street is a prime example.

In 1992, eight historic Dallas neighborhoods were placed on the National Historic Trusts list of "11 Most Endangered Historic Places," with Tenth Street being one of the eight.[239] Dallas buildings to make that list over the years are the Dallas Courthouses in downtown, the Texas Centennial Building in Fair Park, and the Statler Hilton Hotel in downtown.

This media coverage, along with strong community preservationist support, helped Tenth Street receive official historic district status in 1993, which according to the historic preservation ordinance meant "existing original and historic structures must be retained and protected." The historic

---

238. Bcworkshop, *Neighborhood Stories: Tenth Street*, 48.
239. "America's 11 Most Endangered Historic Places—Past Listings," National Trust for Historic Preservation, accessed October 1, 2020.

overlay (boundary) narrowly defined the Tenth Street neighborhood to the area between Clarendon Drive to the south, I-35 to the west, Eighth Street to the north, and the homes bordering Moore Street to the east. According to the survey submitted for the ordinance, thirty-nine buildings were either vacant, boarded-up, or under demolition order at that time.[240]

One of those buildings was the Sunshine Elizabeth CME Chapel (also known as the Elizabeth Chapel)—the oldest Black church in Oak Cliff, founded in 1889.[241] David Perry remembered how "the stained glass windows cast a beautiful light and color that shone over the pulpit… giving it a feeling of exhilaration and holy space, where God [was]."[242] The chapel fell victim to decreased attendance, disrepair, and abandonment in the late '80s as the neighborhood declined.

Perry, Boswell's great-great-grandson, intervened.

He helped lead an effort to restore the chapel in 1995 after nearly two decades of abandonment. One urban planner described the chapel as reaching "a point of desperation. One good ice storm or windstorm [away from coming down]." After repeated attempts to restore and save the chapel, the roof eventually collapsed, and the building was torn down. The northeast corner of I-35 and Tenth Street lays barren to this day.[243]

―――――

240. City of Dallas Department of Planning and Development, *Planned Development District for the Tenth Street Neighborhood* (Dallas, TX: City of Dallas Department of Planning and Development, 1993), 7.

241. Norma Adams Wade, "Trying to Preserve the Past—Area Residents Work to Save Neighborhood," *Dallas Morning News*, February 13, 1995. Larry Powell, "After Awhile, Playing the Heavy Wears a Little Thin," *Dallas Morning News*, March 14, 1995.

242. *Buildingcommunityworkshop*, "Neighborhood Stories: Tenth Street."

243. Wade, ibid.

Structural Battles

Elizabeth Chapel's distinctive wooden folk gothic style caught Robert Swann's attention in the early '90s when he returned home to Dallas after earning his architecture degree. The distinctive wooden square spires rose above the church and were easily visible to commuters on I-35. Robert told me he meant to go take a closer look at the church but put it off because he "didn't really see the urgency at the time." Robert wouldn't return to Tenth Street for over ten years.

On a whim one afternoon in early July 2008, Robert purchased a light rail day pass and headed down to check out the neighborhood. "I was dismayed by how little was left," Robert remembers. He learned it was a freedmen's town only the year before. As Robert walked the winding Tenth Street that day, he happened upon an abandoned house. He would spend the next seven years fighting the City of Dallas to purchase and restore it.

The house's owner died a few years prior. Robert found a slip of paper with a phone number in the back of a bible he found in the house. Miraculously, the number was still connected and the search began, turning into a family history quest for living heirs to the deceased owner.

Amidst frustrating legal battles with the City of Dallas to gain rights of the property and structure, Robert was slowly uncovering deeds, documents, and other narratives from the house and the neighborhood. He learned the house was built in 1896 by a master carpenter in the neighborhood. The Boswell family's importance in the neighborhood came to light in his research, and he found significant evidence that property for the neighborhood was purchased by freed slaves, rather than given away.

Eventually, Robert gained ownership of the house in 2015, nearly connecting the house's entire chain of custody in the process. Protecting one structure in Tenth Street took seven years. Getting a structure demolished in Tenth Street takes considerably less time.

Saving Tenth Street

Twenty-six years after Tenth Street received historic designation, the neighborhood was again placed on the National Trust for Historic Preservation's "11 Most Endangered Historic Places" in 2018.[244] Patricia Cox wrote, petitioning the National Trust for help in saving the historic neighborhood. It is currently considered the most intact freedmen's town remaining in the *country*. The exaggerated demolition rate is putting that distinction to the test.

Since being registered as a historic district, over a third of the 260 structures contributing to the district designation are no longer standing.[245] This information still makes me pause. I struggle to wrap my mind around how losses like that could take place in a historic neighborhood. It's pretty clear when you look at the way the City of Dallas ordinance was written.

As of 2010, if a residential structure in a Dallas historic district is under three thousand square feet, an accelerated

----

244. "Discover America's 11 Most Endangered Historic Places for 2019," National Trust for Historic Preservation, May 30, 2019.
245. City of Dallas Department of Planning and Development, *Planned Development District for the Tenth Street Neighborhood*, 7.

demolition process can be applied to such homes.[246] This qualification requires the home to be considered a "public nuisance" in order to receive accelerated demolition status.[247] Section 51a-4.501(i) of the City of Dallas building code, which Robert repeated to me by memory, was enacted in 2010. City attorneys argued the need to quickly "eradicate blight from beleaguered neighborhoods."[248] This is a common refrain we have heard throughout Dallas's history and across the country.

"Public nuisance" and "blight" are vague terms leaving significant room for interpretation.

For broader Dallas context, primarily White historic districts are the only districts in Dallas with residential structures three thousand square feet or larger.[249] When we consider the context of the circumstances, many of the homes in Dallas's freedmen's towns, like Tenth Street and North Dallas, were built by newly freed slaves or families coming out of generations of slavery, with relatively modest means. Predominantly White historic districts saw fifteen demolitions across eight neighborhoods between 1993 and 2017.[250] Three times that many homes (seventy-two) were

246. City of Dallas, "The Dallas City Code Section 51A-4.501(i) 'Certificate for Demolition for a Residential Structure with No More Than 3,000 Square Feet of Floor Area Pursuant to Court Order,'" American Legal Publishing Corporation, accessed March 26, 2021.

247. Ibid.

248. Robert Wilonsky, "Dallas Eyes Ways to Spare the Historic Tenth Street District, Which Is Now on a National Most-Endangered List," *Dallas Morning News*, May 30, 2019.

249. City of Dallas, "The Dallas City Code Section 51A-4.501(i)."

250. Erickson, "Positive News, for Once," Candy's Dirt. City of Dallas Office of Historic Preservation, "City of Dallas Demolition Delay Log," Demolition Delay Overlay Districts, accessed October 1, 2020.

demolished in Tenth Street over the same time period, a comparatively disproportionate rate of demolition.[251]

Demetria McCain and Jennifer Rangel work for the Inclusive Communities Project, a fair housing advocacy nonprofit. Focusing on organizing and informing neighborhood across Dallas, it has worked to advocate with the Tenth Street neighborhood to protect their history from continued demolition. Rangel notes, "If equity is a value in [Dallas], we need to have an acute awareness of the impact of our City ordinances."[252] I completely agree.

The evidence in Tenth Street suggests how significant the ramifications of seemingly small city policies can be. Zoning designations or the square footage in a demolition ordinance can have ripple effects exacerbating decline in a community. As Jennifer Rangel suggests, it is crucial for all residents in a city to be aware of the ordinances and policies shaping land use in our neighborhoods.[253] For my own part, I will no longer pass a sign reading "Proposed Rezoning" without stopping to see what is being built or how the use may change, even if only out of curiosity.

For neighborhoods like Tenth Street, there is more than curiosity on the line. Preservation of the organic historical and genealogical nature in one of the most intact freedmen's towns in the country is an imperative.

Robert Swann describes the nature of Tenth Street as being a lot like the organic and conversational development of American Jazz. Tenth Street wasn't about star architects or anything like that. It was about "houses that spoke to each

---

251. Ibid.
252. Rangel, ibid.
253. Ibid.

other, the way jazz musicians speak to each other."[254] Robert said, "You can no more understand Tenth Street by preserving a single house than you can understand American jazz by preserving a single note."

———

While Tenth Street may be a neighborhood with a history of cuts, those cuts do not define the neighborhood—the history does. Lifelong residents like Lou Nell Sims, Patricia Cox, Shaun Montgomery, and others continue fighting. Clarence Holoman said, "I didn't go to Vietnam and get blown up, shot up, to come back and let somebody take… my family's history. I didn't do that. I'm gonna fight, and I'm gonna fight for this community."[255]

With new I-35 development on the horizon, the fight to protect Tenth's Street history and residents is alive and well. If the bleeding doesn't stop, there will never be a chance to heal.

---

254. Hampton and Swann, ibid.
255. *Buildingcommunityworkshop*, "Neighborhood Stories: Tenth Street."

6

(UN)FAIR PARK

———

Car brochures and cotton candy: those were the only things I cared about at the State Fair of Texas. Bright colors and sweet days off from school, I sat in the driver's seat of brand-new cars, dreaming of the day I would one day be able to drive. I imagined a future on the road. If asked to recollect past State Fairs of Texas, I could only tell you about the auto shows.

Aside from the occasional overnight lock-in at the Museum of Natural History as an elementary school student, I spent very little time thinking about the area around Fair Park, where the State Fair is held every fall.

As I grew older, I realized I was definitely conditioned to think, similarly regarding Deep Ellum, that Fair Park was a place you didn't linger if you were headed south of downtown. I didn't consider how Fair Park and the Fair Park neighborhood were separate places with their own distinct histories. Without thinking critically about the place, I only frequented a handful of times out of the year and I accepted things as they were because my memories confirmed the narratives I needed them to.

As with every Dallas neighborhood covered so far in this book—and countless others not covered—neighborhood narratives require both an active curiosity to research and a willingness to deconstruct personal narratives in order to better understand.

Fair Park is no different.

The Early Days and the KKK in Dallas

Chartered in true Dallas fashion, the State Fair of Texas intended to celebrate the history and development of Dallas. The Dallas State Fair Association selected a nine-person committee to head up organizing the first event in the fall of 1886. Disagreement about location of the Fair arose almost as soon as the group came out of the starting gate. As a result, two fairs were held the first year: one in north Dallas (on land then owned by John Cole, the first surveyor in Dallas), and one in southeast Dallas (on land which was owned by William H. Gaston, who was instrumental in the H&TC and T&P railroads making their way into Dallas).[256]

After running both fairs at essentially the same time, the fairs barely made enough money to cover expenses. State Fair Association supporters on both sides decided it best to combine efforts and hold a single fair event on the eighty-acre Gaston property going forward. Fair Park occupies the same space today, albeit much larger at 277 acres.[257]

256. Clint Skinner, "Fair Park: History & Overview," Texas Escapes, August 28, 2016, accessed December 20, 2020.

257. Ibid.

The Fair was a strictly White affair at the outset. It would take another two years, in 1888, before Dallas's Black citizens would have a day to attend the fair on Colored People's Day: the second Monday in October.[258] After Colored People's Day 1910, Black visitors were no longer allowed into the fair.[259]

Ku Klux Klan members took control of elected state and local leadership (police commissioner, district attorney, judges, sheriff, etc.) during the 1920s. Dallas had the largest Klan chapter and highest per capita membership in the country during this time.[260] In 1923, Dallas Klan No. 66 held a "Klan Day" at the Fair. Klan Day saw 160,000 Klan members from across the state and country pass through with over 5,000 men and women inducted as new members to the order in front of an audience of 25,000.[261] Then and now, nearly one hundred years later, Dallas works hard to distance itself from this legacy.

---

258. Rachel Northington Burrow, "Juanita Craft: Desegregating the State Fair of Texas," *Legacies* 16, no. 1 (Spring 2004): 19.

259. Peter Simek, "The Long, Troubled, and Often Bizarre History of the State Fair of Texas," *D Magazine*, September 26, 2019.

260. Terry Anne Schulte and Marsha Prior, "'We Return. We Return from Fighting. We Return fighting.' Post-World War I Freedman's Town/ North Dallsa, 1919-1930," in *Freedman's Cemetery*, eds. Duane E. Peter, Marsha Prior, Melissa M. Green, and Victoria G. Clow (Plano, Texas: Geo-Marine, Inc., 2000), 154.

261. Ibid. Peter Simek, "The Long, Troubled History." Obed Manuel, "Why the State Fair of Texas Sucks: Its history is Super Racist!," *Central Track*, September 29, 2017.

The Hall of Negro Life

Not to be outdone by Houston and San Antonio, Dallas business leaders influenced the City of Dallas to put up $3.5 million in appropriations, winning the bid to hold the Texas Centennial Exposition in 1934.[262] The park would see an expansion of one hundred acres and fifty buildings in the next two years. Architect George Dahl was selected to design the buildings and chose the popular art deco style to embody the progressive era. Fair Park now stands as one of the largest collections of art deco buildings in the world and one of the most intact and unaltered World's Fair sites in the United States.[263]

The Centennial Exposition made space for a broad range of Texas cultures including the Hall of Negro Life. Jesse Thomas, general manager for the exhibit, recalled being "stunned and humiliated to the 'nth' degree when word finally reached them that no appropriation had been made by either the City of Dallas or the State of Texas providing for Negro participation."[264] Withholding the appropriation was an act of retaliation toward the Black community for seeking political representation.

Ammon Scott Wells was the first Black resident to run for Congress in Dallas in 1935. A Congressional seat became available due to a court appointment that year, and Wells was one of sixty-five candidates to run. White city leaders considered a Black candidate disruptive to the social order of the city. Several White city leaders threatened to cut the proposed

262. Jesse O. Thomas, *Negro Participation in the Texas Centennial Exposition* (Boston: The Christopher Publishing House, 1938), 59.
263. Patrick Sisson, "Fair Park, an Art Deco Icon in Dallas, May Be Due for Big Change," *Curbed*, December 5, 2016.
264. Thomas, ibid., 59.

one hundred-thousand-dollar appropriation for the Hall of Negro Life if Wells continued his candidacy. Wells refused to back down and he was able to mobilize enough votes to finish sixth in the large field, losing by just nine hundred votes.[265]

City and state funding was withheld anyway.

The one-hundred-thousand dollar building and exhibit instead received funding from the federal government due, in large part, to the lobbying efforts of the Dallas Black Chamber of Commerce and A. Maceo Smith. The building took just three months to build and was dedicated to service on Juneteenth 1936.[266] Operations of nearly one hundred employees were managed by Jesse Thomas and A. Maceo Smith, selected by a Congressional Centennial Committee.

Four hundred thousand visitors are estimated to have visited the exhibit over the five-month exposition the *Dallas Morning News* billed as a "History of Negro from Jungles to Now to be Shown."[267] Overt racism aside, the exhibit was an astounding success. Participation covered thirty-two states and the District of Columbia and included thousands of individual exhibits.[268] These exhibits showcased from education, social service, business, and agriculture to art and music, including an outdoor concert by Duke Ellington.[269] Thomas described the exposition as,

265. Darwin Payne, *Quest for Justice: Louis A. Bedford and the Struggle for Equal Rights in Texas* (Dallas: Southern Methodist University Press: 2009), 32.
266. Juneteenth is the day slaves in Texas learned of the Emancipation Proclamation, 6/19/1865. Paul M. Lucko, "Hall of Negro Life," Texas State Historical Association Handbook of Texas, accessed August 10, 2020.
267. "History of Negro from Jungles to Now to be Shown," *Dallas Morning News*, May 14, 1936.
268. Paul M. Lucko, "Hall of Negro Life."
269. Thomas, ibid., 62.

"[possibly] the largest collection of books written by and about Negroes ever assembled in one building (227)... painting(s)... sculpture(s)... dioramas, miniature farms, maps which showed the distribution of farm population, farm implements made and manufactured by Negroes... charts [showing] the growth of business... photographs and personal [histories] of Negroes who [argued] important cases before the different state supreme courts and the Supreme Court of the United States..."[270]

Later that year, Negro Achievement Day would be reintroduced at the State Fair, and Black residents would be allowed to fully participate in Fair activities for the first time since 1910.[271]

Success for the exhibit would be short-lived, though, as the Hall was demolished in 1937—just a year after its construction. Demolition approval came from the exposition commission chaired by future mayor of Dallas Robert Lee Thornton without consulting the Black Advisory Committee.[272] The Greater Texas & Pan-American Exposition was to open later that year to highlight the achievements of the twenty-one countries across the continental Americas (South, Central, and North).[273] The understanding was that the Hall of Negro Life would be included as part of the new event;

---

270. Ibid., 30-35.

271. Kathryn Siefker, "NAACP Youth Council Picket Line, 1955 Texas State Fair," Bullock Museum, January 2015, accessed December 10, 2020. Peter Simek, "The Long, Troubled History."

272. Robert Lee Thornton is the namesake of the Dallas portion of I-35E in Dallas. Will Maddox, "Early Influencers: Robert Lee 'R. L.' Thornton," *D Magazine*, January/February 2020. Thomas, *Negro Participation*, 124.

273. Steven Butler, "Greater Texas & Pan-American Exposition: Introduction," Historic Fair Park, accessed March 10, 2021.

however, the exposition commission passed the following resolution on December 30, 1936:

> "After careful consideration, we do not feel that the Negro building would be of any value to the new Exposition… the new Exposition will need the space now occupied by the temporary Negro Building. I have also had the matter up with the City of Dallas and they do not care for the Negro Building, therefore it seems best, in the light of circumstances, that the Negro Building be abolished."[274]

The Hall of Negro Life was the first and only Centennial building demolished. Subsequently, the Negro Hall of Achievement land that was going to be utilized for new Central and South American exhibits lay vacant, unlike the exposition commission had described.[275] Adding insult to injury, the leveled space became a parking lot for a Whites-only swimming pool—a pool that would be filled with concrete when segregation ended, ensuring Blacks and Whites would never have to share it.[276]

---

274. Thomas, *Negro Participation*, 122.
275. Ibid., 123.
276. At present, the site is home to the African American Museum of Dallas, restoring the space back to Black Dallasites. Robert Wilonsky, "Fair Park Hasn't Always Been Fair to Everyone, and It's Time Dallas Finally Tells That Story," *Dallas Morning News*, April 19, 2019.

Segregation at the Texas State Fair

For another thirty years after the Centennial Exposition, Black presence in the Fair continued to be segregated. Black residents were allowed to attend every day but could not fully participate in exhibits and rides, as these were activities restricted to Negro Achievement Day. The State Fair acted as a microcosm of broader Dallas segregation.

Juanita Craft was largely to thank for turning the tide of segregation at the State Fair in 1967.

Craft's life in advocacy began in her early thirties upon joining the National Association for the Advancement of Colored People (NAACP) in 1935. As a field organizer, Craft was a force to be reckoned with. She and Lulu Belle White were responsible for canvassing the state and establishing 182 NAACP branches in Texas.[277] Craft described herself as a "young hothead" in her early organizing years picketing and staging sit-ins.[278] Her fire and persistence gained her the distinction of being the first Black woman to vote in an election in Dallas County in 1944.[279]

Craft's interactions with the State Fair started in 1955 as she began organizing peaceful protests against the annual Negro Achievement Day.[280] Craft and the high school students she organized with boycotted outside Fair Park's art deco gates at 7 a.m. on Monday, October 17, Negro

277. Mamie L. Abernathy-McKnight, "Craft, Juanita Jewel Shanks (1902-1985)," Texas State Historical Association Handbook of Texas, accessed December 10, 2020.

278. Frederick Murphy, "Juanita Craft and Her Persistence," *History Before Us*, accessed December 15, 2020.

279. Ibid.

280. "Dallas Protests," The Anti-Apartheid Movement in North Texas, accessed September 1, 2020.

Achievement Day.[281] Their hand-painted signs read "TODAY IS NEGRO APPEASEMENT DAY AT THE FAIR" and "Don't Sell Your Pride for a Segregated Ride."[282] Craft recalled in a 1974 interview, "Kids were on top of people's houses along the route of the parade with megaphones telling about the segregated policy [at the fair] and to stay out."[283] While the day of picketing and boycotting may not have led to immediate desegregation of the Fair, it catalyzed the change process.

The State Fair made partial steps over the next twelve years as Craft's boycotting and picketing continued: Negro Achievement Day became Achievement Day in 1957. Four years later, Achievement Day ended, and October 17, 1967, marked the full integration of the Fair. Craft's continued fighting led to full rights of enjoyment for Black citizens within the Fair after eighty years of operation.

Expanding Fair Park

Outside the gates of Fair Park, the surrounding neighborhood saw the Dallas disinvestment machine in action.

In 1959, Dallas city planners recommended the majority Black Fair Park neighborhood just south and east of the park grounds be acquired for use by the State Fair of Texas. Condemnation was threatened but was never put into action. Without public notice, expansion plans for Fair Park were

281. Ibid.

282. Rachel Northington Burrow, "Juanita Craft," 21.

283. Michael L. Gillette, "The Craft of Civil Rights," Humanities Texas, February 2010, accessed November 10, 2020.

revised several times during the '60s and came to a head in 1968 when the City began buying property. Fair Park homeowners were upset that the City of Dallas did not hold public meetings informing them of the plans. This would have at least provided context to why the City suddenly began acquiring property through eminent domain.[284]

Eminent domain is considered a legal right under the Fifth Amendment of the US Constitution. In general, it is the right of the government to seize property and transfer from private to public ownership but not without *just compensation* to the landowner.[285]

While the City of Dallas was performing Fair Park expansion studies, an internal moratorium was placed on permits within the expansion study area. This meant no improvements were approved for plats within the neighborhood, potentially leading to lower property values.[286] Without public notice of the moratorium, it is possible Fair Park residents were unaware this was officially sanctioned.

Residents hired Austin-based Urban Research Group (URG) to perform independent land appraisal analysis to ensure the just compensation they were offered was indeed *just*. URG's investigations confirmed the permit moratorium in Fair Park. URG found City of Dallas Building Inspection

284. Elizabeth Durham Davies, "Fair Park Expansion: A Case Study of Political Bias and Protest in Urban Politics" (master's thesis, North Texas State University, 1974), 16-17.

285. In 1875, Kohl v. United States was the first eminent domain case heard by the Supreme Court. Many of these early eminent domain cases condemned property for construction of public buildings, building aqueducts for drinking water, and maintenance of waterways. For example, the Kohl case involved construction of a federal customs house and post office in the City of Cincinnati. "Fifth Amendment," Cornell Law School Legal Information Institute, accessed November 1, 2020.

286. A plat is a plot of land.

Department documents revealing every map with a plat in the Fair Park neighborhood had "a penciled instruction dated August 7, 1968, 'no permits be issued except those for wrecking and moving purposes.'"[287] It appears the City of Dallas attempted to deflate home values, actively disinvesting in neighborhood improvements in order to obtain land at a lower price, expanding Fair Park for a lesser cost in the process.

Additionally, spot zoning was used as a technique to disrupt the primarily residential makeup of the Fair Park neighborhood, eventually morphing into a mix of residential, multi-family, retail, and commercial uses.[288] Little Mexico experienced similar zoning impacts three and a half miles northwest from Fair Park around the same time.

This pattern of injustice jumped out at me in the process of revising this book. Rereading Fair Park narratives with a better understanding of zoning and Little Mexico's history made the connection between the two neighborhoods more evident. Spot zoning began evidencing itself as a tool consistently and systematically used by the City of Dallas to influence land use and redevelopment in Black and Brown neighborhoods. Operationally, this decreased land use values in neighborhoods where redevelopment was on the agenda.

———

287. Davies, "Fair Park Expansion," 18.
288. Multi-family housing includes duplexes and apartments. Davies, "Fair Park Expansion," 17-18.

"If you just..."

Two years before URG's investigation and analysis, in November 1966 a report titled "A Redevelopment Plan For The State Fair of Texas" was produced for the State Fair of Texas by the Economic Research Association. The report's goal was finding improvements in the State Fair experience. Appendices in the report provide information from a group interview conducted as part of the research. Group members were chosen at random from people visiting the Fair in the past five years.[289] While not explicitly stated in the report, it is reasonable to assume voices of color were not as well represented, if at all, based on the group's responses. Some of the comments included in the report read:

"Fair Park is a lovely place... but you feel uncomfortable."

"You don't feel safe *around* fair park."[290]

"I know you're not supposed to discuss race and discrimination... but, anyway, to me that's the main problem of the Fair right now"

"... if the racial problem didn't exist you wouldn't feel bad about going to that bad part of town."[291]

Later on in the interview, the panel was asked, "If all the land around Fair Park were bought up and turned into a paved, lighted, fenced parking lot, would that solve the problem?" The Dallas citizens "answered with a resounding 'Yes,'" confirming the City of Dallas's plans to purchase land around the park.[292]

---

289. *A Redevelopment Program for the State Fair of Texas: Prepared for State Fair of Texas November 1, 1966* (Los Angeles: Economic Research Associates, 1966), A-3-5.

290. Emphasis added.

291. *A Redevelopment Program for the State Fair of Texas*, A-3-5.

292. Ibid.

"The solution for all of these conflict... is simple," the Economic Research Association claimed. "All that is required is to eliminate the problem from sight. If the poor Negroes in their shacks [could not] be seen, all the guilt feelings... will disappear."[293]

When a friend told me about this report, I didn't believe it existed. I mean, I wasn't going to be surprised if it did—history has taught me better by now. I wanted to believe average residents of Dallas would do better, knowing full well policies are shaped by representation and public opinion. I remembered Dr. Marvin Dulaney's James Baldwin quote in reference to "Negro removal." Dallas citizens wanted to remove Black Fair Park residents and homes because they "did not project the image of [a] prosperous, progressive and pleasant Dallas."[294]

(Un)Fair Market Value

Black Fair Park homeowners continued fighting for equitable fair market value housing appraisals, after they were originally offered an appraised value of $0.65 per square foot for their homes. White homeowners in the area were reportedly receiving appraisals as high as $4.17 per square foot, 540 percent higher than Black home appraisals.[295] These exceedingly high valuations included one home owned by White City

293. Ibid., A-5.
294. For more information on coded language, see Chapter 8: Space, Place, Justice. Davies, "Fair Park Expansion," 17.
295. Marlyn Schwartz, "City Unfair, Fair Park Citizens Say," *Dallas Morning News*, February 4, 1969.

Council member Abe Meyer.[296] After continued back and forth with City Council, Black home appraisals rose to $0.75 and eventually $1.00 by mid-1969 after residents continued raising opposition.[297]

For present context, one dollar in 1969 is equivalent to seven dollars in 2020.[298] If the average home size in Fair Park was one thousand square feet, the undervaluing of Black Fair Park homes would equate to present day loss of twenty-one thousand dollars in value.

On June 30, 1969, two hundred protesters in support of the Fair Park homeowners crammed inside City Council chambers to push council action on either fair market value or proceed with condemnation, hoping the courts would look favorably on the homeowners.[299] City Council indeed took action and decided to begin condemnation hearings a month later, ten years after the first notification in 1959.[300]

A young Civil Rights leader named Rev. Peter Johnson arrived in Dallas in late 1969 on the orders of Andrew "Andy" Young, his boss at the Southern Christian Leadership Conference (SCLC). Rev. Johnson explained to me, "Dallas was the last place I wanted to be." The city was written off as hostile to the Civil Rights movement. Coming from a man who shed blood in Alabama, Mississippi, Louisiana, and Texas and still suffers internal injuries from walking the Edmund Pettus Bridge in Selma, Alabama, that's saying something.

---

296. Ibid.

297. Davies, "Fair Park Expansion," 29.

298. "US Inflation Home," US Inflation Calculator, accessed January 20, 2020.

299. Carolyn Barta, "Court to Decide Fair Park Prices," *Dallas Morning News*, July 1, 1969.

300. Carolyn Barta, "Fair Park Action OK'd," *Dallas Morning News*, August 2, 1969.

In fact, his sole purpose for coming to the city was getting the *KING* documentary screened and to bring the proceeds back to Atlanta to support the newly widowed Coretta Scott King, wife of Martin Luther King, Jr. SCLC leadership wanted him "to get in and get out, with the money."[301]

With the *KING* documentary approaching rapidly the following March 1970, Johnson recalled that, as the youngest member of the group, he had "a lot of pressure riding on his shoulders." Dallas was the only city in the world refusing to screen the documentary. Yes, you read that right—in the world.[302]

White theater owners refused to show the film, and Black theater owners were afraid to show it.[303] Rev. Johnson had access to a thirty-minute promotional preview of the movie he had seen with other Civil Rights leadership in Atlanta. With the help of Herbert Howard, pastor of Highland Park Baptist Church, Rev. Johnson worked out a deal where, "if [he] could get the [preview], [Howard would] invite the right people to be there." "[Rev. Howard] couldn't guarantee that it was gonna be a good experience... but [he could] get them there," Rev. Johnson remembers.

"Once the lights came back on, there wasn't a dry eye in the church," Rev. Johnson said. "All of those rich, powerful, powerful men were literally in tears."

Soon after Rev. Johnson arrived in Dallas, local advocates, like Al Lipscomb, felt the need to bend his ear. They had seen

---

301. Jim Schutze, "To Get Fair Park Right, We Have to Get the History of Fair Park Right," *Dallas Observer*, July 5, 2016.

302. Dallas' White and Black leadership were not welcoming to Martin Luther King Jr. In fact, King is only reported to have given two appearances in Dallas.

303. Jim Schutze, ibid.

his success in swaying the White power structures of Dallas to premiere the *KING* documentary. Johnson's nonviolent political strategies had proven themselves capable of enacting change within the city. This was an area the Fair Park homeowners found themselves grinding to a halt, thanks to the at-large representation system on the City Council. Without direct neighborhood representation and only one Black representative, George Allen, on the Council, there was little progress made through the traditional political process—tactics needed to change.

Rev. Johnson was due back in Atlanta forty-eight hours after the premiere of the documentary. He asked to stay for another month to work with the Fair Park homeowners and Andy Young said, "No, you can't. You better get your ass back here and get on a plane, the ticket has already been paid for." Rev. Johnson did not return to Atlanta.

Instead, Rev. Johnson stayed and met with the homeowners in the basement of Mt. Olive Lutheran Church and remembers crying listening to their stories.

Rev. Johnson provided me an example of what he heard from the neighborhood group based on the land value appraisal research they were getting back from URG. It was a pattern of discrimination based on race. For example, if a Black family was living at 1401 4th Street and had a 150-by-100-foot lot and a three bedroom, one bath wood-frame house, they may receive an appraisal of fifty cents per square foot. Next door at 1403 4th Street, there could be an identical lot and home with a Black family renting the home from a White landowner. The research showed that property received an appraisal of one dollar per square foot higher than the Black owned lot.

"It was mostly African American senior citizens who bought their homes through the GI Bill... these were little shotgun houses, but these were people's homes," Rev. Johnson said. "We knew we could not win against eminent domain—that's constitutional. We would have to win on fair market value."

Dallas Mayor J. Erik Jonsson refused discussing any requests from the Fair Park homeowners. "We fought Bull Conner in Birmingham and he wasn't as sophisticated a racist as the mayor of Dallas," T. Y. Rogers of the SCLC remarked about Jonsson.[304] On New Year's Eve 1969, facing the threat of a six-hundred-person picket line at the nationally televised Cotton Bowl Parade the next morning demanding desegregation of the parade, Mayor Jonsson agreed to meet with Rev. Johnson.

Rev. Johnson told the mayor he needed to meet with the residents and not himself. So, "we headed down to the mayor's office, Al Lipscomb, J. B. Jackson, Mrs. Elsie Faye Higgins, Don Johnson," Rev. Johnson recalled. As they rode up the elevator to the mayor's office, Rev. Johnson prayed with them and told them, "I don't want to talk to the mayor, I want y'all to do it... it shouldn't be done by someone from outside. Y'all need to look him in his fucking face... and tell him these are your homes."

Mayor Jonsson agreed to a meeting to discuss the fair market value of their homes and to stop condemnation proceedings.[305] Rev. Johnson pushed the homeowners to ask for desegregation of the parade as well. J. B. Jackson rode with the mayor in the parade the next morning, desegregating the Cotton Bowl Parade for the first time in history.

304. Judy Wiessler, "SCLC Plans Major Effort in Land Fuss," *Dallas Morning News*, May 17, 1970.
305. Davies, "Fair Park Expansion," 35.

The meeting was scheduled for February 1970; Mayor Jonsson cancelled and pushed back to May.[306] The New Year's Eve meeting staved off the Cotton Bowl protest, saving Dallas's face on national television, but the meeting never materialized any meaningful action on behalf of the homeowners. Throughout May, talks broke down between the mayor and the Fair Park homeowners, and condemnation proceedings were reinstated that month.

Twenty-eight homeowners were angered by the lack of follow-through by the mayor and decided to take the City of Dallas to court. Homeowners cited the injustice as a legal matter over due process and their eminent domain rights.[307] Residents argued the proper procedures were not followed by the City of Dallas in the course of taking their property because no notice was given. The neighborhood group worked with the American Civil Liberties Union to file a federal suit in *Joiner v. City of Dallas* in the fall of 1970.

After the homeowner's case was dismissed by the federal district judge Joe Estes, the Fifth Circuit Court of Appeals upheld Judge Estes' motion. This meant the neighborhood had no other legal option except to appeal to the Supreme Court in the fall of 1971, where the case sat for an unprecedented year and a half before being heard by the court. When action was taken in the spring of 1973, the Supreme Court

---

306. Ibid., 36.

307. Due process is defined by Merriam-Webster as "a course of formal proceedings carried out regularly and in accordance with established rules and principles." Essentially, due process is a legal requirement that the state must respect all legal rights owed to a person, a fair shake. *Merriam-Webster,* s.v. "due process (*n.*)," accessed December 10, 2020. "Due Process," Cornell Law School Legal Information Institute, accessed December 10, 2020.

sent the case back to the Fifth Circuit Court of Appeals where it was finally heard in 1974 by judge Sarah T. Hughes.[308]

Rev. Johnson was absolutely correct.

The neighborhood could not and did not win on eminent domain procedural rights. In fact, the *Joiner* case is now used as a reference for the lack of procedural justice at the state level in carrying out eminent domain processes.[309] As of 2010, only twelve states provided full due process protection before taking land through eminent domain, and Texas is not one of them.[310] The Supreme Court ended its ruling on the case with the following summary:

> "We have concluded that the sum of the stigmata detected in the Texas eminent domain statutes does not total constitutional deficiency. This means only that these statutes do insure to property owners their minimum rights under well-established interpretations of the Fourteenth Amendment. We cannot compel more than this, for the Constitution is not a blueprint for the heavenly city."[311]

Plainly, the Court agreed that the Constitutional bar was low but Texas and the City of Dallas did not fail their Constitutional requirements. It was a lose-lose for the neighborhood. The land was legally taken by the City of Dallas without the need for a prior hearing and land values were not equitably

---

308. Davies, "Fair Park Expansion," 87.

309. D. Zachary Hudson, "Eminent Domain Due Process," *The Yale Law Journal* 119, no. 6 (April 2010): 1300.

310. Hudson, "Eminent Domain Due Process," 1322-23.

311. "Joiner v. City of Dallas, 380 F. Supp. 754 (N.D. Tex. 1974)," Justia US Law, accessed October 16, 2020.

priced for all property owners, leaving big questions about just compensation and fair market value.

Again, we must ask ourselves: who holds the power in determining the use of the land?

———

Today, Fair Park and the surrounding neighborhood remain in a state of tension. Rightfully placed distrust between the neighborhood, the City of Dallas, and the State Fair of Texas remains a wound in much need of healing. It has not helped that the Fair continues purchasing land surrounding Fair Park. As recently as 2009, the Fair purchased $549,000 worth of land in the surrounding neighborhood.[312] Much of the land owned by the Fair sits bulldozed and vacant.

As third-generation Fair Park resident Ashley Walker put it, "[The Fair builds] on people's land and houses, and they move them to build parking lots. It make you feel like they're robbing you from where you've been all your life, you and your family. Someone you know is gone and there's just concrete. They're taking it away and there's nothing you can do—to make more parking lots for their Texas-OU games."[313]

Jim Schutze is the author of the incredibly controversial history of Dallas's racist past, *The Accommodation*, and long-time critic of White power structures in Dallas. He argues Fair Park is one of the only parks in Dallas that has the opposite effect on the surrounding neighborhood: instead

---

312. Robert Wilonsky, "Wilonsky: How the State Fair of Texas Turned Its Own Neighborhood into a Giant Fair Park-Ing Lot," *Dallas Morning News*, May 3, 2016.

313. *A Great Park for a Great City* (Dallas: The Foundation for Community Empowerment, 2017), 11.

of the park bringing property values up, it brings them down. It's an interesting consideration, especially because the housing stock in Dallas increased by 72 percent between 1970 and 2013 and decreased by 50 percent in Fair Park. Property values in the rest of the city increased four times faster in the rest of the city between 1999 and 2014.[314]

This shouldn't be a surprise given that Fair Park's existence has proven hostile to the surrounding neighborhood.

However, there may be some hope left for the park and neighborhood after all. Fair Park First is the nonprofit arm overseeing the management and stewardship of Fair Park as of 2018.[315] They've worked hard *with* the community on developing a master plan for the park. In June 2020, the Fair Park Master Plan Update was presented to the Park Board. In stark contrast to the improvements carried out fifty years ago, Fair Park First heard from over five hundred community voices as part of their research for the plan, and it shows. Park Board President Calvert Collins-Bratton said in an interview with the *Dallas Morning News*, "We cannot fail these neighbors who have lobbied and advocated and poured blood, sweat and tears into this area for so many years and gotten only empty promises."[316]

The proposal's first phase includes adding over fourteen acres of green space and will rip up the parking lots and fences along the western edge of the park to create a community park tying into the neighborhood. Anna Hill, a Fair

---

314. Jim Schutze, "New Report Tells Sordid Past of Fair Park, State Fair of Texas—but Offers Hope," *Dallas Observer*, August 3, 2017.

315. "Who We Are," Fair Park First, accessed March 10, 2021.

316. Sharon Grigsby, "Decades after Dallas Stole African American Homes, Master Plan for a Better Fair Park Gets OK," *Dallas Morning News*, June 22, 2020.

Park neighborhood resident, says, "That's a lot better than a lot of cement... Those trees and lawns are what Fair Park should have had in it a long time ago."[317] For a neighborhood that lives the other 341 days of the year without Fair patrons, perhaps the park will finally become a neighborhood asset.

---

317. Ibid.

7

A CASE FOR REFRAMING OUR HISTORY

———

"You rarely change things by fighting the existing reality. To change something, build a new model that makes the existing model obsolete."

—BUCKMINSTER FULLER

Learning to tie your shoes in a new knot is really difficult. We spend years learning how to tie our shoes so they fit just right. We don't think too much about wearing shoes on our feet—they become a part of who we are. You might not even think about tying those knots now, it just happens. You may not even remember where you learned the motions in the first place (I know I can't). Yet, our shoelaces still manage to come untied and trip us up... and we tie the same knots again and again.

Because that's what we do. "It's how we always do it."

Through my research I have learned that unlearning is just as important (if not more important) than initially learning information. Unlearning requires, and allows space for, reflection on why we do things the way we do them.

Early in my research, I found myself watching a 2018 C-SPAN recording of a panel discussion on infrastructure development… yes, I'm *that* guy. The panel included historians from across the transportation spectrum, from airports to highways. Dr. Peter Norton was one of those panelists and my reason for watching. His opening lines hit me like a hammer:

> "I think that [our] infrastructure future is based on a past we don't understand very well. In fact, more than that, I would say the past we have grown up with about surface transportation (roads, highways, etc.) in this country is a past that was created, in part, to justify the status quo. I don't think we can understand the status quo or how we got there until we reexamine the past."[318]

Norton brings up an important point. When we talk about infrastructure, we usually talk about building something new or fixing something existing. We don't talk much about the past. The narrative often lost is the history of the infrastructure in relation to the people impacted by it. Questions like:

- How did these roads/buildings get there?
- Who designed them?
- What was there before them?
- What needs did they serve?
- Who were they intended to serve?

318. National History Center, "Infrastructure Development," *C-SPAN*, May 4, 2018, video, 1:01:48.

All of these are questions of the past, bygone days, days that couldn't possibly be relevant to anything in the present context, right?

Norton's argument resonates with me as I stumble through the *learning, unlearning, and relearning* journey I've embarked on. I try to wrap my head around decisions I made as an engineer, and that the City of Dallas made in the past. I have worked hard while creating this book to get all of the information correct, to hear the right voices—only to find out I still know relatively little and had a backward understanding. Some people call this "conscious incompetence."

I don't think this is reason to stop engaging with the past. In fact, I think it is the very reason to further pursue history and bring it forward into the present. Learning, unlearning, and relearning is the essence of narrative change.

History can often be treated as a burden—and ignored as such. This is an easy trap to fall into. I know I dealt with this notion of ignoring versus understanding many times while trying to redesign pressure stations on pipelines: I wanted to erase the old piping and replace it with new, pretending the old station never existed. It took significantly more effort to understand why the station was designed a certain way and to learn from the past designs. Just as we are products of our own upbringing, I would argue that infrastructure also wears its history in ways we may or may not see.

Dr. Norton's views on the importance of understanding the historical context of infrastructure were shaped in his twenties while working for the Historical Society of Delaware in Wilmington during the 1980s. Surrounded by photographic negatives from 1910-60 in the basement of a former bank building, Peter saw glimpses of Wilmington's past. The negatives were reverse images in more than one sense: they revealed a city drastically different from the one he saw on his bus ride home from work.

I read about this experience in the introduction to Dr. Norton's book, *Fighting Traffic*, and had the chance to talk with him about this period. In our conversation, he noted that he first felt "like a resident alien in [his] own country" because he was "an adult but not a driver." As Peter rode the bus home each day, it became clear to him what values were designed into the world around him. "And that gave me a perspective, where it was quite obvious that the world was designed on the assumption that you have a car... so that was very personal."

What he saw in the photographs was a Wilmington that no longer existed—particularly, predominantly Black areas of Wilmington that were more or less paved away into parking lots, roads, and driveways. "The verb that came to my mind then was 'erased'—like they took a big rubber eraser and erased it. But... 'paving away' is clearly what it was," Norton recalled.

It was at this intersection (no pun intended) of personal and imagined experiences where Dr. Norton saw a "striking contrast to what [he] was getting from the literature... the engineering literature was pretending that this was all objective engineering." Further, Dr. Norton said, "Once you build a certain boundary around what you can consider, it starts to make *internal* coherence, but it makes no *external* coherence." You create an echo chamber.

Peter saw a disconnect between the historians and what he encountered in primary sources. Historians treated infrastructure expansion as an inevitable response to car culture, building a boundary around what could be considered.

Dr. Norton's curiosity narrowed in on city streets. Mainly, he wanted to understand where the shift in the nature of streets went from caring for the pedestrian to caring for cars and drivers. In my experience, from an early age, the street was typically approached with caution. It was an accepted fact. "Look both ways before crossing the street," they would say. It never occurred to me questioning this narrative was an option. Thankfully, it occurred to Peter.

As many historians would, Dr. Norton researched works spanning the past century gathering together a broad narrative. He found significant opposition to the coming age of the automobile in his primary sources. We often hear stories where the automobile was welcomed with open arms, a savior of humanity. The research showed the dominant social norm of walking and crossing streets was becoming an impediment to the needs of the automobile—a wide street.

Early twentieth century streets were often crowded, busy, and filled with multitude of transportation types (pedestrians, railcars, horse and buggy, etc.)—a negative narrative increasingly touted by city officials, engineers, and the auto industry. Amidst the fights for pedestrian safety and automobile rights came a shift in the status quo.

In the United States, the turn of the twentieth century saw an increasing number of automobile-related injuries and fatalities to pedestrians. Pedestrians banded together to shape the public safety movement, even going so far as erecting monuments to memorialize children killed by automobiles and holding Safety Week parades, which likened drivers of automobiles to Satan.[319] Definitely no miscommunication there.

The auto industry, anonymously referred to as *motordom*, used stylized models by Bel Geddes to paint a picture of a future enriched by the automobile. Shell Oil's "City of

---

319. Peter Norton, *Fighting Traffic: The Dawn of the Motor Age in the American City* (Cambridge: The MIT Press, 2008), 38-45.

Tomorrow" and GM's prophetic "Futurama" exhibits at World's Fairs introduced people to the idea that superhighways were only twenty years away—that 1960 was within reach: automobiles moving around freely, at great speed, with pedestrians nowhere in sight. The automobile was not the problem—pedestrians and people were the design flaw: a foolproof highway was motordom's manifesto.[320]

The manifesto eventually manifested. Many, not all, US cities saw the Interstate Highway System crisscross the country and infiltrate their urban cores, dividing up neighborhoods in the name of safety, efficiency, traffic relief, and the American Dream. The road narrative was rewritten over a thirty- to forty-year period by a combination of automotive interests and public policy coupled with strong public relations. We bought into the self-fulfilling prophecy that we needed automobiles to be full participants in the American story and had a duty to support whatever infrastructure made that happen.

We still see these influences today with popular engineering assumptions that adding more lanes will reduce traffic when they can actually create more.[321] The continuation of our inherited highway and infrastructure legacy impacts the ability for infrastructure to be used for other purposes and remain resilient in the face of changing conditions. As Norton told me, "If you start off with the wrong theoretical approach, it doesn't matter how meticulous you are—you will remain trapped."

---

320. Ibid., 249.

321. Induced demand/traffic applies the traditional supply and demand theory to transportation planning. The theory suggests increasing the lanes on a road or highway reduces the "cost" of driving and encourages more trips, inducing demand.

Norton's book opens with an epigraph from a 1922 issue of *Engineering News-Record*. A quote at the bottom of a section titled "Motor Killings and the Engineer" reads, "the obvious solution… lies only in a radical revision of our conception of what a city street is for."[322] Norton feels hope in the sense that if we were able to shift the social construction of the street into one dominated by automobiles, then there is hope that we can change it again. I'd like to think we are just at the beginning of a new cultural shift as well.

"We had a legacy before of vast quantities of urban rail networks… so, even infrastructure can change. I think what has to change first, is the ideology behind the infrastructure," Norton said. Fundamental narrative shift goes beyond "questioning the details, you have to question the fundamental assumptions."

"Just like how Copernicus… had to question the fundamental assumption that the earth is the center of the universe, and only then could the other things get worked out," Dr. Norton recalled. Our work of creating more equitable cities follows a similar trajectory.

By challenging our fundamental assumptions, smaller assumptions and actions that tend to perpetuate systems of injustice can surface and be examined, allowing for transformation of ourselves and our cities. I think the words of writer and activist Audre Lorde capture this sentiment well:

"… the master's tools will never dismantle the master's house. They may allow us to temporarily beat him at his own game, but they will never enable us to bring about genuine change."[323]

---

322. "Motor Killings and the Engineer" (editorial), *Engineering News Record* 89, November 9, 1922, 775.

323. Audre Lorde, *The Selected Works of Audre Lorde*, ed. Roxane Gay (New York: W. W. Norton & Company, 2020), 41.

Critical reflection of our assumptions shifts the historical narrative from "this is how we've always done it" to "this is how we did it" and toward "this is how we're going to undo it and rebuild it." For that, we need a different set of tools.

No more tying the same knots—we need different shoes.

———

Ahead

As we move into this next section of the book, we will explore and attempt to answer these questions:

- What words are we using to describe people and place?
- Why is this practice continued over and over?
- When and how are community members involved in a design process?
- Who is being displaced? Why?
- Who is carrying out design and implementation?
- Which variables and voices are we considering most important in development?

II

REDESIGN

———

8

SPACE, PLACE, JUSTICE

"Space is not an empty void. It is always filled with politics, ideology, and other forces shaping our lives and challenging us to engage in struggles over geography."

—EDWARD SOJA, *SEEKING SPATIAL JUSTICE*

"This past weekend it was over ninety degrees in Chicago. It was great weather for backyard barbeques, going to the local park, or just sitting out on the porch." Mary Pattillo, Harold Washington professor of sociology and African American studies at Northwestern University, depicted a memory of an afternoon beach trip she took in her South Side neighborhood in a 2016 Urban Institute policy debate. She further described the scene:

> "Given Chicago's notoriously racially segregated geography, it was mostly Black, but there were also a number of Latino and Asian families among the crowds. I watched kids make sandcastles, throw footballs, splash in the water, and eat hot dogs and potato chips. All

along the grassy parkland families put up tents, laid out blankets, played cards, and told jokes. The air was thick with barbecue smoke. Teenagers flirted, checked their cell phones, played cool and got loud, sent video chats, and danced. Bikers and walkers tried to maneuver through toddlers and old people wandering onto the path… And then I got an email that a student who attended the charter school where I serve on the board had been shot and killed on his block."[324]

Pattillo describes how the last sentence describing the afternoon fits the characterization of Chicago's South Side neighborhoods "[reversing] the weight of the evidence [she] just recited" previously. "… The second one-sentence paragraph overshadows all of [the positive imagery] with the painful (and unacceptable) reality of death. Our labels follow suit. We neglect all of the assets and emphasize the challenges," Pattillo asserted.[325]

I'm just as guilty of this type of characterization in my own writing and understanding of Dallas. In some ways the previous chapters highlight a lot of negative impacts to those neighborhoods, potentially furthering a negative portrayal, outweighing the description of positive voices and aspects of the neighborhoods. How we think and talk about the places we live and don't live matters.

We must rebuild our theories, understandings, and language of space, place, and justice.

———

324. Nancy La Vigne, "The Power of Language: Rethinking How We Talk about Place," *Urban Institute*, accessed January 17, 2021.

325. Ibid.

Give Me Some Space!

Hearing the word "space" probably conjures up mental images of the moon, stars, wide open fields, or the lofty ceiling of a big-box store like Sam's Club or Costco. Perhaps space is more personal, evoking notions of reading nooks, bedrooms, or the distance between two people, especially as the COVID-19 pandemic created a greater awareness of what six feet looks and feels like. Rather than thinking about space as something passive that exists all around us, creating space is instead an act we all engage in.

Space is an action, where something occurs.[326]

Author and architect Craig Wilkins describes this reconception of space in his book *The Aesthetics of Equity: Notes on Race, Space, Architecture, and Music*. Wilkins began what is known as the Hip-Hop Architecture movement. As he describes it, he was searching for a way to represent a Black vernacular in architecture because representation of Black architects in the profession is around 2 percent.[327]

Wilkins saw a connection between the way the hip-hop movement took something passive like a turntable and transformed it into an active instrument in the music creation process. "Taking things that were designed for one thing and adapting and using them for something else is a spatial condition as well," Wilkins describes. "You take a space that was designed for one thing and you use it for something else, because you don't have anything else." Through this lens,

---

326. Craig L. Wilkins, *The Aesthetics of Equity: Notes on Race, Architecture, and Music* (Minneapolis: University of Minnesota Press, 2007), 97-115.

327. The Detroit News, "Craig L. Wilkins on Hip Hop Culture and Architecture," Facebook, October 22, 2017.

Wilkins flips architecture from a noun into a verb.[328]

Architecture moves beyond simply the buildings that surround and envelop us and into a creative process of engagement and interaction with each other.

In *Aesthetics of Equity*, Wilkins breaks down our construction of space traditionally defined by Western thinking and reconstructs the idea through layering in thoughts from three other philosophers. Below, the first example is how space is traditionally thought of (passive), followed by three new concepts of space (active), building on each other.

"A classroom is a classroom because by the label on the blueprint, the sign on the door, and the arrangement of seats and desks we have abstractly defined and limited it as space." (John Locke)[329]

- This could be how we might usually describe space, defined by an outside entity, existing only because it was defined as so. An architect, engineer, or citizen might predetermine how a space is defined based on their viewpoint. Whiteness and colonialism operate from this viewpoint. Conceiving space from this vantage point perpetuates power structures and the ability for space to be defined by those with the power to do so.[330]

"A classroom is a classroom because by teaching there, we have actively made it space." (Henri Lefebvre)[331]

---

328. Ibid.
329. Wilkins, *The Aesthetics of Equity*, 113.
330. Whiteness refers to structures that produce White privilege. Colonialism is a practice of domination, involving the subjugation of one people to another. Wilkins, *The Aesthetics of Equity*, 10-13.
331. Wilkins, *The Aesthetics of Equity*, 114.

- Instead of space being defined in a fixed way ahead of time, Wilkins describes Henri Lefebvre's notion of space as defined by the interaction between people. Space is a social creation, where we gain knowledge of the space by the *interaction of those using it*. Therefore, space is an identity constructed by those engaged in and performing the story.[332] Individuals learning and interacting with each other and the teacher make it a classroom.

"A classroom is a classroom because by teaching there, we have actively made it space, but every classroom in the world ain't for everybody." (Michel Foucault)[333]

- Foucault builds on Lefebvre and agrees interactions between people creates space, and he adds that interactions *between spaces* creates space. I try to understand it through places being clusters: the clusters have interaction internally and between them, but there is space in between that isn't considered part of the cluster. Foucault argues not all spaces are for everyone. This is how segregated Black and Brown neighborhoods are often viewed as outside of the "norm" and described in relation to White neighborhoods.

"A classroom is a classroom because by teaching there, we have actively made it space, but just because every classroom in the world ain't for everybody, don't mean it ain't all good." (bell hooks)[334]

---

332. Ibid., 99-100.
333. Ibid., 114.
334. Ibid.

- We often think of marginalized or disinvested communities as spaces away from the center, therefore different, and not necessarily in a good way. bell hooks flips the script on what might be considered "other" spaces by placing them at the center rather than the margin. She inverts the idea entirely. Disinvested and marginalized communities become spaces of possibility where identity is created through defining space on their terms.[335]

For hooks, space liberates rather than oppresses.

This last expansion by bell hooks moves the conversation of marginalized spaces and people from one of comparison to the norm toward space that is "the standard, the norm, the model by which all *other* things are judged."[336] Wilkins translates hooks's revolutionary description of space, especially at the margins, "as sites of activism and empowerment—a space where one can resist having identity thrust upon oneself and create an identity of one's own choosing."[337] Agency.

Space must be the first area where we begin deconstructing hierarchies and perceptions about who defines space and how space is defined. Again, we are all responsible for creating space through our interactions. If we rob spaces of their agency (identity) by attempting to assert control over them from the outside, then there is little chance of moving toward equity. That movement will come through a definition of space from the inside-out rather than the outside-in.

---

335. Ibid., 112.
336. Ibid., 103.
337. Ibid., 104.

Words in Place

Words are powerful. Throughout researching neighborhoods in Dallas and cities across the country, certain words continued to pop up when writers attempted to describe various places: "cancerous," "slums," "blighted," "distressed," "disadvantaged," and "high-crime." Words like these influenced the narratives of places that I had never set foot in.

In my own experience in Dallas, neighborhoods like Deep Ellum and Fair Park were summarized as "high-crime" and "poverty-stricken," even though I knew that no place could be described with just a few words or phrases. I didn't describe my own neighborhood that way. Similar to Pattillo's South Side of Chicago example in the opening of this chapter, a single event has the potential to mar an entire story, an entire neighborhood, an entire city.[338]

I am aware that I use some of this biased, overgeneralized language in this book—I am still learning. Throughout the revisions process, I have attempted to change some of these descriptions, but it is impossible to completely remove my bias from my writing. Perhaps one of the most telling things about language is that the words someone uses to describe a place will always be two-fold—the person will always be both describing the place itself and their relationship to the space.[339]

───────

338. Nancy La Vigne, "ibid.

339. Jennifer S. Vey and Hannah Love, "Recognizing That Words Have the Power to Harm, We Commit to Using More Just Language to Describe Places," *Brookings*, July 13, 2020.

[Deficit] + [Geography]

We often use biological terms like "cancerous" and "blighted" in an attempt to describe how an area functions within the larger body of a city. This is called transference: modifying a term and passing meaning from one context to another.[340] Jennifer Vey and Hanna Love at the Brookings Institute argue "language about *place* matters, because it can be used to justify actions taken toward *people*."[341] By using clinical language, we distance ourselves and start to view people and places as problematic, as opposed to the systemic racism and classism itself.

Take the word "slum," for example. In the early twentieth century, this word was used to describe areas that were underfunded and didn't have paved roads, running water or sewers. Neighborhoods were reduced to (and defined by) their shortcomings. No one heard about the amount of community and economic development occurring in spite of these challenges:

- Strong community bonds and mutual aid
- Small business development
- Thriving cultural centers
- Tight knit family units

People also didn't hear about the multitude of factors leading to these negative conditions to begin with:

- Residential redlining
- Racial and economic segregation

---

340. *Merriam-Webster*, s.v., "transference (*n.*)," accessed February 16, 2017.
    Brentin Mock, "The Meaning of Blight," Citylab, February 16, 2017.
341. Vey and Love, ibid.

- Inadequate city services and utilities
- Land use/zoning/permit manipulation
- Lack of political representation[342]

No, neighborhoods were just "slums."

Vey and Love say the shorthand to describe communities often looks like a "combination of 'deficit' plus 'geography' (e.g., distressed places, struggling neighborhoods, etc.) to describe communities impacted by racism, disinvestment, physical destruction, and economic exclusion."[343]

Words also become harbingers for policy solutions and grant funding. This is especially the case in areas described as "slums" or "blighted," which became targets for "slum clearance" and urban renewal policies.[344] Deficit-based language was reinforced through early federal public housing policies aimed at "clearing slums" to create new public housing. Unfortunately, a "slum" is not a clearly defined criteria and thus is open to interpretation and application, often leaving those in power to justify use as they see fit.[345] If an area was described as "blighted" then it provided justification for use of urban renewal and eminent domain policies to clear land and people in communities of color.

Rather than describing an individual property or experience, words like "blight" are applied at the neighborhood level, effectively ostracizing an entire area in the process. Using these vaguely negative terms to describe neighborhoods can

---

342. Ibid.

343. Ibid.

344. Justin Garrett Moore, "Why We Need a New Word for 'Blight'," Medium, October 8, 2015. Joseph Schilling and Jimena Pinzon, *Charting the Multiple Meanings of Blight: A National Literature Review on Addressing the Community Impacts of Blighted Properties* (Blacksburg, VA: 2015), 10-12.

345. Vey and Love, ibid.

further the perceived inability of an area to be given funding or have any opportunity at investment, as this language implies that the area is beyond repair.[346] I would argue that the terms we use to describe places is what is truly in need of repair.

———

Naming It

Vey and Love share a framework they use in their own research to combat these biases in their place-based language:

- Be intentional about the implication "place" language has for people
  - Minimize stigma, acknowledge harm, recognize agency of people within places
- Explicitly name the systemic root causes behind conditions, inequities, and challenges within places
- Be specific, strengths-based, and solution-oriented
  - Refer to unique histories, strengths, and contemporary contexts to inform solutions[347]

This kind of change in our language doesn't happen overnight. Stigmatizing and oppressive language carries centuries of precedent and bias with it.

One thing I have attempted to do in this book is highlight the specific elements that contextualize neighborhoods and

———

346. Ibid.
347. Natalie Spievack and Cameron Okeke, "How We Should Talk about Racial Disparities," Urban Wire: Race and Ethnicity, February 26, 2020. Vey and Love, ibid.

residents in Dallas within the racist discriminatory policies and history that created disparities. At times this was easy to do, though other times it was more difficult. I often wanted to shy away from sharing the history and experiences of people of color out of fear of misrepresentation or missing a part of the narrative. At the same time, I knew those unique individual histories were a critical component to recognizing the agency within the neighborhoods. It would have been easy to rely on statistics and to present information in a theoretical fashion. I almost abandoned some chapters because I was too afraid about getting something wrong and perpetuating a stigma.

Perfectionism is a characteristic of White supremacist culture.[348]

Natalie Spievack and Cameron Okeke say, "Talking honestly about racism carries risks… and naming the structural causes of racial disparities can make some uncomfortable and drive them away."[349] Being comfortable is a privilege, especially for White people largely unaffected by the specific policies and impacts outlined in this book.

Conversations about the causes of systemic practices need to be approached "with informed thoughtfulness, but abandoning the discussion altogether creates a void that perpetuates harmful narratives and prevents finding solutions."[350] Silence says more than a book ever can. Much like Craig Wilkins's description of space, reconstructing our language of place is an active endeavor.

This is an opportunity to move forward, lean into that uncomfortableness, and become curious.

---

348. Tema Okun, *White Supremacy Culture*, (dRworks, n.d.), 1.
349. Spievack and Okeke, ibid.
350. Ibid.

And I ask you to ask yourself: what makes you uncomfortable while reading these narratives?

Designing Justice with Bryan Lee

Design justice questions and evaluates elements of power and place, suggesting that design has the ability to communicate power.

Think about something as simple as a bold font, easily commanding your attention. Tall buildings command a large presence in a downtown space. Multilevel highway interchanges communicate that the road is the most important thing, and you receive that message from miles away. Their presence is not lost on the communities around them.

"The design profession is an institution, and like all institutions it imposes its power and leverages privilege through the component systems that make up the institution."[351] Bryan Lee's framework for justice stems from his childhood and the sharp contrast he experienced moving from Comiso, Sicily, to Trenton, NJ:

> "[Comiso, Sicily] in itself was one of the most beautiful places I've lived in my entire life. I remember walking through the streets and plazas and falling in love with this place. Sometimes with the people, sometimes with the architecture. When I was twelve, things changed a

---

351. *Form Function Studio*, "Design for Everyone: An Intro to Design Justice," August 24, 2020, video, 1:20:09.

little bit… I don't know if you've ever been to Trenton, NJ, but I was not in love with the architecture of this place… it was kind of in the hood."[352]

Living in New Jersey with his grandmother for a time led to his understanding of the relationship between humans and space. He describes the long, narrow staircase running through the middle of his grandmother's house as an "abyss," one his grandmother painfully traversed all day long to merely navigate her house. Lee thought to himself, "My grandmother shouldn't live in a place where the architecture hurts her body."[353]

The dissonance between those two cities gave birth to an understanding of what disadvantage and disparity looked like; of how different spaces and places could affect the humans that inhabited them.[354]

Space and place. These were the areas Lee felt he could make an impact in the communities around him. Justice was the thing allowing him to serve the community he was a part of, understand communities he was not a part of, and to have a purpose in design beyond himself and about the specific context. Lee writes that "Design Justice seeks to dismantle the privilege and power structures that use architecture as a tool of oppression and sees it as an opportunity to envision radically just spaces centered on the liberation of disinherited communities."[355]

This lens on justice helps frame architecture as a language where the built environment tells our stories. For Lee, "culture

---

352. *TEDx Talks*, "Race, Architecture, and Tales for the Hood l Bryan Lee l TEDxTU," April 22, 2016, video, 9:13.
353. Ibid.
354. Ibid.
355. Bryan Lee, "America's Cities Were Designed to Oppress," Citylab, June 3, 2020.

incubates in our cities, neighborhoods, and blocks as a consequence of the persistent circumstances and immediate conditions."[356] Architecture is not a lone actor in this regard—we are all responsible for creating space and speaking the language.

"We have to consider the signals and the receivers we are sending out and catching," Lee says, illustrating how design communicates with the world around us. Imagine on one end of a spectrum you have *signals*, things like pedagogy, policy, and procedures. Signals tell us how the world *should* be ordered and constructed. On the other end of the spectrum are *receivers*, things like practice, projects, and people. Receivers take in information from signals and respond. Signals and receivers are not passive entities or components of the design institution. They actively participate in creating and perpetuating systems, most perniciously when racial bias is involved.[357]

The Signal			The Receiver		
Pedagogy	Policy	Procedure	Practice	Project	People
The defining process of indoctrinating theoretical and conceptual ideas of a practice or profession, generally in an academic environment.	A regulatory statement of intent, and is generally performance-based. Policies are generally adopted by a governance body and passed onto an executing body to establish procedures or protocols to carry out the intent of the policy.	The prescriptive sequence of actions or instructions established for the governing body to carry out the intention of policy initiatives.	A conventional, traditional, or otherwise standardized methodology of operating, by the governed, in response to or in accordance with policies and procedures set forth by a governing body.	Something that is devised, planned. An undertaking, small or large, that has direct implications in or for the positive emotional or physical well-being of the users in the built environment.	The individuals and communities that make up the constituent population. Often times subject to the prevailing forces of the process and relegated to a reactionary position unless actively organized and engaged.
Ideology	Codification	Implementation	Methodology	Realization	Culture

Table 1. Design Impacts From Signal to Receiver[358]

---

356. *Form Function Studio*, "Design for Everyone: An Intro to Design Justice," August 24, 2020, video.
357. Ibid.
358. Ibid.

Lee sees opportunity for active participation at every degree of the signal-receiver spectrum. Failing to participate is how "privilege and power are able to, whether wittingly or unwittingly, marshal these systems to maintain power."[359]

---

359. Ibid.

9

PATTERN FOR A JUST CITY

"In short, no pattern is an isolated entity. Each pattern can exist in the world, only to the extent that is supported by other patterns: the larger patterns in which it is embedded, the patterns of the same size that surround it, and the smaller patterns which are embedded in it. This is a fundamental view of the world. It says that when you build a thing you cannot merely build that thing in isolation, but must also repair the world around it, and within it, so that the larger world at that one place becomes more coherent, and more whole..."

—A PATTERN LANGUAGE

When I first learned that the bodies of 1,157 formerly enslaved people were moved to build a highway in Dallas, my shock refused to believe it. Frantic research led me deeper into the understanding of the North Dallas neighborhood, when I learned about Roseland Homes, which expanded my lens beyond just transportation and into housing and urban renewal policy. These infrastructure elements I found in North Dallas became the foundation for a pattern I began seeing in other neighborhoods in Dallas.

As I began learning and relearning about other neighborhoods in Dallas, these infrastructure and policy patterns became clearer. Researching North Dallas to Little Mexico to Tenth Street was like reading the same story over and over—a story about a White-controlled city slowly dismantling neighborhoods of color. While each neighborhood has its own unique context and history, the broader patterns of systemic racism are evident within each neighborhood.

Of the five neighborhoods of color we covered:

- Four dealt with a highway or road widening coming through the neighborhood
- Four had public housing projects located in or near them[360]
- Four dealt with zoning and/or eminent domain issues.

Once you begin to see the patterns, it's difficult to unsee them. My own day-to-day experience of Dallas is forever changed now. I see the patterns continuing today in Dallas and recognize them in other cities across the country as well. It's a White supremacy toolkit.

When we step back and take in the cohesive narrative of Dallas, the patterned injustice toward neighborhoods of

---

360. Public housing in and of itself is not a bad thing, it's a necessary thing. However, the siting of low-income housing in neighborhoods already occupied by people with low incomes can contribute to the concentration of poverty. See the Supreme Court case Texas Department of Housing and Community affairs v. Inclusive Communities Project, Inc. for more information.

color becomes readily apparent. The more specific we are in our understandings of racism and injustice, the easier it is for us to identify and work toward correcting systemic issues.[361]

Patterns

I was introduced to *A Pattern Language* through several social media accounts in the summer of 2020. Luckily, the SMU library had a copy available and I could check out the hefty, fragile, red book, which—according to a note on the inside cover—was missing pages 1109-1140. The due date slip on the back cover showed signs of sporadic use over its forty-three-year life, sometimes going almost six years without being checked out.

A Pattern Language is the first book of a three part series dedicated to providing a "complete working alternative to our [then] present ideas about architecture."[362] Through the use of words, drawings, and photographs, the authors uncover patterns "[describing] a problem and then [offering] a solution that enables professionals and residents to collaboratively improve a city, neighborhood, or building" based on the identified pattern.[363]

---

361. See "Words In Place," "[Deficit] + [Geography]," and "Naming It" sections in previous chapter.
362. Christopher Alexander, Sara Ishikawa, and Murray Silverstein, *A Pattern Language: Towns, Buildings, Construction* (New York: Oxford University Press, 1977), cover. Toni Griffin, Laura Greenberg, Laier-Rayshon Smith, ed., *Patterned Justice: Design Language for a Just Pittsburgh* (Cambridge: Just City Lab at Harvard Graduate School of Design, 2020), 64.
363. Toni Griffin, Laura Greenberg, Laier-Rayshon Smith, ed., ibid., 64.

The authors take a network approach toward understanding the ways cities are built out and identify sequences inherent within those networks.[364] They view the sequence of patterns as both a summary of the language and an index of the patterns.[365]

Patterns help us reflect on questions like: How do we understand our interaction with the world around us in our daily lives? In what ways do elements of a neighborhood interact with each other? What elements do I continually see?

Further, patterns encourage us to pose questions about how injustice replicates in our cities: Which neighborhoods experience the most/continued displacement? Have we taken the time to observe, research, interview, and catalogue them? And how might we create a new pattern language of justice and equity?

―――

Take a Seat

Imagine the ways a large network structure like a city or town is created by elements in shopping centers, streets, bike paths, meeting rooms, staircases, and chair placement. All of those patterns are the foundations of our interaction with the world—they are the pattern language for our lives.

For example, the 252nd pattern in *A Pattern Language* highlights different chairs as a pattern to replicate. The authors note states, "People are different sizes; they sit in different

―――

364. Network approaches building relationships around a shared vision.
365. Christopher Alexander, Sara Ishikawa, and Murray Silverstein, ibid., xviii.

ways. And yet there is a tendency in modern times to make all chairs alike."[366] Anyone who has ever been uncomfortable in a classroom growing up or sitting in a chair at a conference or community meeting can probably relate to this experience.

What we end up with is an average chair that works for some body types yet ultimately leaves other people uncomfortable. Size differences aside, the repeated use of an identical chair within a space also gives the impression the intended action is to sit (i.e., a teacher or company is defining how the space will be used and interacted with). This has the potential of leaving out important distinctions like: How long people are sitting? Are people engaging in a heated discussion, just chatting, or are they sitting for a few minutes in passing?[367] This potentially creates a lack of diversity in interaction with the space because seating options are inevitably limited as are the interactions supported by those options.

When I think of the classrooms I occupied, especially in junior high and high school, they were all very rigid in their design: rows and rows of square desks with an arm rest on one side and open on the other. It's a ubiquitous and universal signal for "classroom." However, learning is a unique and individual process, and the same pattern of chairs is not necessarily conducive to all subjects and learning types.

Research on classroom environments is beginning to show a shift in thinking about the layout of traditional classrooms. A study in the UK in 153 elementary schools showed a 16 percent improvement in student scores when moving them from the least effective to the most effective classroom.[368]

---

366. Ibid., 1158.
367. Ibid.
368. Peter Barrett et al., *Clever Classrooms: Summary and Report of the HEAD Project* (Manchester: University of Salford, 2015), 15.

Researchers found that the flexibility of the classroom layout to allow for more stimulation, individualization, and natural features promoted a more positive learning experience for a greater number of children. The study acknowledged that simply changing the chairs and furniture would also need to be paired with a change in teaching to accommodate the new classroom layout and increased interaction with students.[369] In the end, a new set of patterns developed for improving learning spaces and facilitating the learning process.[370]

Each small pattern, like the size and placement of a chair, builds up into a coherent language of a classroom or a city, a language that creates dialogue with those interacting with it. Living could be seen as a two-way conversation between people living in a home, city, or region and the streets, buildings, parks, and other infrastructure. My daily interactions with the road as I drive to work, the door as I enter a building, or a trail while I exercise in a park are all part of a larger conversation. This discourse in our personal environments helps us understand the public and private realms existing in our lives and furthers our understanding of how cities may be patterned toward injustice.

Some examples of these patterns of injustice can be seen in the first portion of this book: highways bisecting neighborhoods of color and walling off communities, street flow patterns influencing driving behavior, zoning changes impacting development, demolition policies allowing for rapid removal of historic structures, and disinvestment in infrastructure and economic development are a few of the common patterns across Dallas' history.

---

369. Stephen Merrill, "Flexible Classrooms: Research Is Scarce, but Promising," Edutopia, June 14, 2018.
370. Barrett et al., *Clever Classrooms*, 38.

Patterns of displacement and erasure permeate our past and present, informing each other as part of a broader city narrative.

Patterns are just the tip of the iceberg, and we must be careful to note that these are hypotheses that are context specific.[371] Each pattern has its own unique set of patterns feeding into and out of it, and the system of patterns must be understood within their individual context. While the patterns in North Dallas, Little Mexico, and Tenth Street were similar, they are individual neighborhoods with their own unique characteristics and pattern languages. To apply a one-size-fits-all lens of understanding could very well end up perpetuating a different pattern of injustice in the process. Patterns are not a rigid framework but a guide to understanding and engagement with the world around us, allowing for critical reflection in our day-to-day movements.

A Just City

"I know you people are trying to move me out of my house, right?" Toni Griffin and her team were asked as they met with Detroiters in 2010. The Detroit Future City planning process was just beginning the planning phases of trying to revitalize Detroit and, understandably, residents were already anxious. At the time, Detroit just suffered a 25 percent loss in population in the housing and auto industry collapses of the early 2000s. In five years, the city would file for Chapter 9 Bankruptcy. "Detroit had become a poster child for an

---

371. Toni Griffin, Laura Greenberg, Laier-Rayshon Smith, ed., ibid., 64.

American city in crisis," Griffin remarked.[372]

Griffin admits she is no stranger to working in contested cities. Her urban planning and architecture career has spanned Chicago, IL, Harlem, NY, Washington, DC, and Newark, NJ, all cities that have plenty of "unresolved issues related to urban justice, issues of equity, inclusion, and access."[373] The work speaks for itself as *Architect Magazine* headlined an interview with Griffin titled "Can This Planner Save Detroit?"[374] While the headline may catch attention, Griffin feels no one person, or single planner, is able to save a city on their own.[375]

Her ideas of urban injustice were formed growing up on the South Side of Chicago in the 1960s, right after the passage of the Civil Rights Act of 1964. Growing up, Griffin "rarely saw or interacted with a person who didn't look like [her]."[376] She witnessed firsthand how segregation laws altered the spaces around her and states that those changes shape how she interacts with cities today. Those ideas also informed her framework for urban injustice, which she defines through three key conditions and patterns:

1. Concentrated poverty
2. Disinvestment, crime, and the architecture of fear
3. Socioeconomic division[377]

---

372. Toni Griffin, "A New Vision For Rebuilding Detroit," Filmed September 2013 in New York, New York, TED video, 11:37.

373. Ibid.

374. Fred A. Bernstein, "Can This Planner Save Detroit?," Architect, October 6, 2010.

375. Ibid.

376. Toni Griffin, "Defining the Just City Beyond Black and White," The Nature of Cities, October 23, 2015.

377. A defensive and alienated stance toward the world, informed by society's preoccupation with fear. Ibid.

Griffin highlights how "spatial segregation has created pockets of concentrated poverty in our cities that, in turn, have created spatial and social isolation of those cities' residents."[378] Based on census data from 2000-18, the number of people living below the poverty line in the City of Dallas has increased by approximately 40 percent, with a population increase of less than 8 percent.[379] Poverty is also concentrated along race and ethnic lines, similar to the redlines originally drawn in the 1930s by the Home Owners Loan Corporation. Neighborhoods like Tenth Street and Fair Park have pockets of concentrated poverty within them, due to generations of disinvestment.

In the context of our conversation, disinvestment, crime, and the architecture of fear manifest in the ways federal programs brought funding for the redevelopment of communities. Most infamously, as we've seen, those programs were under the umbrella of Urban Renewal or the Interstate Highway System. Dallas was a recipient of millions of dollars of federal funding for these programs. The programs helped clear homes and build highways right through the urban core. This is a common refrain across the country, especially in neighborhoods of color, or at least where they used to be.

Griffin is working to get us singing a different refrain. As with any language, she notes, "[We] must first create a clear definition of what it means to have [a] just city."[380] In an essay contribution for the first volume of *Just City Essays*, Griffin shares her ten values for a Just City:

---

378. Ibid.
379. Regina Montoya and Mark Clayton, "Mayor's Task Force on Poverty Update" (PowerPoint presentation, presented to City of Dallas Human and Social Needs Committee, May 7, 2018).
380. Toni Griffin, "Defining the Just City Beyond Black and White," The Nature of Cities, October 23, 2015.

- Equity
- Choice
- Access
- Connectivity
- Ownership
- Diversity
- Participation
- Inclusion
- Belonging
- Beauty
- Creative Innovation[381]

These elements form the foundation of a new pattern language that is critical for her mission to heal and repair cities experiencing injustice. Again, the most important takeaway is that each community will need to define and develop its own values of just cities—there is no one-size-fits-all approach.[382] This is why Griffin and her team at the Just City Lab at the Harvard Graduate School of Design created the Just City Index.

In 2017, the Just City Lab investigated the definition of urban justice and injustice. From their home in New York City, Griffin's team examined "how design and planning contribute to the conditions of justice and injustice in cities, neighborhoods and the public realm."[383] The Just City Index serves as a catalogue of values helping communities articulate their own visions of a Just City: a values-driven pattern language for just design and planning.[384] All ten of Griffin's

---

381. Ibid.
382. Ibid.
383. The Just City Lab, *Just City Index* (New York: The Just City Lab, 2017).
384. Toni Griffin, Laura Greenberg, Laier-Rayshon Smith, ed., ibid., 63.

Just City values are included within the list, plus another forty conditions for justice. The expanded conditions include notions of ownership, durability, vitality, spontaneity, delight, reconciliation, protection, equity, togetherness, voice, and agency, just to name a few.[385]

The Just City Lab works with communities to not only identify values present in their current context but what values the community envisions for its future. Each community is unique and must develop its own understanding of where it is and where it wants to be—a personalized dialect of justice.

Patterned Justice

In the fall of 2019, Griffin led a design studio class at the Graduate School of Design titled "Patterned Justice," which applied the Just City Index methodology to the city of Pittsburgh, PA. The intention of the studio class was "to explore the scale and repetition of urban spatial and social conditions that contribute to why marginalized communities do not have full access to the systems, spaces, and supports that bring about full economic participation and wellbeing."[386] At a more granular level, the class performed an analysis similar to the case studies in the first half of this book, identifying the specific and cumulative impacts certain neighborhoods experience.

---

385. The Just City Lab, *Just City Index.*
386. Toni Griffin, Laura Greenberg, Laier-Rayshon Smith, ed., ibid., 63.

Recognizing the "scale and repetition" of patterned injustice in our own cities gives us an opportunity to redesign them with justice in mind. Griffin explains that "thoughtful, community-informed design can have a role in dismantling—and facilitating—solutions to the physical, social, economic, or environmental systems and structures that are at play in making our cities unjust."[387]

Working in partnership with the residents and community partners in Pittsburgh, students in the studio worked to understand patterns of injustice existing within four specific neighborhoods experiencing historic disinvestment: Beechview, Hazelwood, East Liberty/Garfield, and the Middle Hill District.[388] Several neighborhoods experienced a lack of investment in infrastructure like sidewalks and stairs, vacant schools, public parks on contaminated land, limited public transit options, and highway and rail barriers dividing the neighborhood.[389]

What grew from the collaborative work was an examination of fifty patterns of injustice within the neighborhoods across three broad categories: in the space of the public, neighborhood change, and mind, body, and soul. The fifty patterns identified within these categories received

---

387. Toni Griffin, "Designing Cities for Justice With Toni Griffin, 'Patterned Justice' Co-Editor & Harvard's Just City Lab Lead Innovator," September 22, 2020, in *We Can Be* produced by Grant Oliphant, podcast, MP3 audio, 32:18.

388. Toni Griffin, Laura Greenberg, Laier-Rayshon Smith, ed., ibid., 71.

389. Pittsburgh is an incredibly hilly city and has many City managed stairs throughout neighborhoods. The highway and rail barriers dividing Pittsburgh neighborhoods are similar to those described in North Dallas, Deep Ellum, Little Mexico, and Tenth Street, except railroads in the present are not as easily traversed and spatially act more like highways.

new proposed *patterns of justice* to combat each injustice. Here is an example from the proposals in the Pittsburgh neighborhoods:

- **From:** highway barriers **to:** green crossings:
  - Beechview neighborhood has beautiful natural amenities going unutilized due to a highway barrier in the community. By creating a green crossing over the highway, the possibility exists to not only connect the neighboring communities but increase proposed bike, pedestrian, and wildlife flow over the barrier. Increased beauty of this crossing may also have a knock-on effect of attracting tourism to this often overlooked area.[390]

As a tool, patterns can be reimagined as intervention tools within a community, perpetuating possibility. Studying the patterns of injustice in Pittsburgh allowed for a better understanding of the underlying conditions that created and upheld systemic injustice. Pattern acknowledgement can potentially create engagement and discussion between policy makers, community organizations, developers, activists, and residents.[391]

Implicitly or explicitly, patterns develop and promote a set of values that shape the cities we live in. Our design languages have created conditions of disenfranchisement and disinvestment in communities. A necessary component of healing those injustices will require a recognition

---

390. Toni Griffin, Laura Greenberg, Laier-Rayshon Smith, ed., ibid., 87.
391. Ibid., 76.

of those patterns and movement toward a collective community-driven reenvisioning and reinvestment in our cities.

As noted in the opening epigraph, patterns are not isolated entities—they are systemically embedded and support each other.[392] Janera Solomon, a consultant/cultural strategist and writer in Pittsburgh's East Liberty neighborhood, sums up the movement forward in this way:

> "We cannot undo or replace without acknowledging. And, it is more than acknowledging that race and class are at the root and have been at the root of urban planning and design. It is acknowledging the intentionality of it all. It's not benign. Not happenstance. Patterns of injustice are 'patterns' because they are repeated. Habitually. If the contemporary conversation acknowledges the pattern without investigating how it came to be and why, then I'm afraid we are going in circles. Or something... worse, reinforcing patterns. Holding patterns in place. But it's complicated. Urban planning has to embrace the complexities. We all do."[393]

As Janera states, recognizing and acknowledging patterns is not enough—it's just the starting point. Developing patterns of justice in our own lives requires active engagement and reflection. That action can be as simple as changing the language we use to describe a place, to something as comprehensive as fixing zoning and land use policies, which negatively impact neighborhoods of color. Einstein is attributed with saying, "Those who have the privilege to know have the duty to act..."

---

392. Christopher Alexander, Sara Ishikawa, and Murray Silverstein, ibid., xviii.
393. Toni Griffin, Laura Greenberg, Laier-Rayshon Smith, ed., ibid., 34.

10

A COMMUNITY VISION

———

"The most dramatic change will not happen through planning processes alone."

—JACOB WOLFF

When we think of community engagement, we often think of a weeknight meeting in a community center or, as Tenth Street Landmark Commissioner Robert Swann put it, "donuts on a Saturday morning." At its worst, engagement can be resigned to a check box: a means to an end, rather than the end itself. At its best, the community drives change and leverages its power, rather than simply being *allowed* to engage in the process.

Sherry Arnstein describes this through the image of a "ladder of citizen participation."[394] At the bottom of the ladder are actions like manipulation, informing, and other forms of "nonparticipation" (e.g., donuts on a Saturday morning).[395]

---

394. Sherry Arnstein, "A Ladder of Citizen Participation," *Journal of the American Planning Association* 85, no 1 (2019): 26.

395. Arnstein, ibid., 26-28.

At the top of the ladder are higher degrees of citizen power like partnership, delegating power, and citizen control. The top rung is where citizens have meaningful power to affect change and outcomes in the decision-making process.[396]

I used to think when I described community development it was a means of leveraging my own privilege to give voice to others. I had my bias checked while reading Barbara Brown Wilson's 2018 book, *Resilience For All*. The opening epigraph of one chapter in her book quotes Detroit resident Sandra Hardy-Taylor:

> "I truly hate [the word 'empower']. No one can empower you. We have the power already. It's just about utilizing that power, and I think… people have been so misled that they no longer think they have this power to really move the city forward. A lot of the work that we have done at this table, in certain communities, we have reenergized that power with the residents. And that is what it's about—reenergizing the power residents already have."[397]

Sandra places the emphasis on assets already embedded in a community, *where the power and voice already exists*. Reading this was a cringey moment for me. I realized my past approach to community engagement was misguided: communities didn't need me to give them a voice—they already have one.

Dallas real estate developer Maggie Parker makes the distinction that prepositions have their own inherent meanings when we note if we are doing work "with" versus "for"

396. Ibid., 31-33.
397. Barbara Brown Wilson, *Resilience for All* (Washington, D.C.: Island Press, 2018), 105.

communities.[398] We must remember that language matters, as it upholds and perpetuates systems of power and privilege. Balancing that dynamic out requires creating opportunities *with* communities to reenergize their power. In this book alone, we've seen several examples of communities who leveraged their power to speak up for themselves. In some cases, that power can move mountains.

―――――

Move That Mountain!

Marsha Jackson moved to a semi-rural area of South Dallas called Floral Farms in the fall of 1995 because it provided space for her daughters to have horses and practice their roping and barrel racing. "It was just a little rural area close to downtown Dallas because I worked in downtown Dallas. At that time, it was a still a small piece of the country still within view of the Dallas skyline."

The area along South Central Expressway is now referred to as a "long stretch of wild west... where, seemingly, anything goes."[399]

In late 2017, Marsha and her family were told the land next door to their home would become a pallet company. Not long after, "[in] January 2018, Blue Star [Recycling] moved there. They started putting concrete right over by my fence, less than fifty feet from my bedroom... and they start this

398. "Growing the Economy—Inclusively," *The Catalyst*, Fall 2019.
399. Robert Wilonsky, "'It's Unacceptable': Why a Dallas Woman Lives Next to Mountains of Ground-up Shingles," *Dallas Morning News*, December 13, 2018.

shingle business." Within a short amount of time, the pile grew into a sixty-foot shingle mountain.

The line of trucks down the road at the McCommas Bluff Landfill can stretch on for miles. As the lowest-cost dumping facility in central Dallas, roofing companies spend a lot of time trying to dump shingles at McCommas Bluff. Out-of-state company Blue Star Recycling began leasing the open space next door to Jackson in order to grind down old roofing shingles into a powder and get roofing companies back on the job by creating a landfill alternative. The ground shingle powder can be recycled into asphalt material.[400]

On the surface, shingle recycling is a noble cause, as it prevents several hundred thousand tons of roofing shingles from ending up in landfills each year (It takes approximately three hundred years for one shingle to fully decompose.). Less than noble are the asbestos and other hazardous air pollutants ground shingles release into the air, or leach into the ground and nearby bodies of water, or the lungs of residents next door.[401]

Jackson noticed she started feeling sick and thought it was merely allergies. An allergy test came back negative. She went one step further and saw a pulmonologist. The pulmonologist told her, "I know it's bad to say this, but it's really not going to clear up unless you move, or unless you die."

Jackson has trouble talking for long periods of time and constantly needs to clear her throat because her vocal cords

---

400. *Blue Star Recycling*, "Blue Star Recycling Dallas Facility," August 29, 2017, video, 9:40.

401. U.S. Environmental Protection Agency. U.S. EPA Innovations Workgroup. *Environmental Issues Associated with Asphalt Shingle Recycling*, by Timothy Townsend, John Powell, and Chad Xu, (Gainesville, Florida, 2007), 11.

are inflamed. Marsha stopped to take a drink of water several times during our interview for this book. When she coughs, her phlegm is black.[402] Her thirteen-year-old granddaughter and her neighbor's three grandchildren do not go outside. "We stay in the house all the time," Marsha told me. "If anyone were ever to go down [her] street, you would never know there were any kids living there."

In February 2018, Marsha began reporting the facility to City Code Compliance anonymously because the shingles "just started stacking up, stacking up at the fence, and knocking the fence down." Frustrated by a lack of response from the city, Marsha said, "Nothing was getting done, so I started reporting [with] my name. And I tried to call my councilman (Tennell Atkins) in March [2018], and he didn't return my phone calls." Those phone calls began a three-year battle to save her health, her home, and her neighborhood.

The Battle

Marsha's land is zoned for agricultural/residential uses, while the land next door is zoned for industrial research uses. Dallas City Council set these land use boundaries in 1989 before Jackson or Blue Star were present, and unfortunately agricultural zoning provides far less protection for residents than single-family zoning does.[403] This is a common occurrence in South Dallas, where industrial zoning is more prevalent,

---

402. Matt Goodman, "The Reality TV Twin Who Built Shingle Mountain," *D Magazine*, August 2019.
403. Ibid.

concentrating hazardous facilities and creating an environmental burden for neighborhoods of color.[404]

Blue Star failed to obtain special use, solid waste, storm water, and pollution permits from the City of Dallas.[405] Marsha finally received a response from City of Dallas Code Compliance and a citation was issued in July and Blue Star shut down temporarily, restarting operation not long after without clearing with code compliance. Eventually, the Texas Commission on Environmental Quality (TCEQ) began an investigation into the six-story, fifty-thousand-pound Shingle Mountain in October 2018.[406] Marsha still hadn't heard anything from her council member, Tennell Atkins, after repeated phone calls and voicemails.

The following month, Marsha attended a meeting for an Environmental Protection Agency (EPA) superfund site in South Dallas at Lane Plating and another meeting just up the road in the Joppa neighborhood where two concrete batch plants were being contested.[407] Marsha connected with environmental activists like Jim Schermbeck and the environmental advocacy organization he founded, Downwinders at Risk.

In December 2018, the coalition building began. Marsha started Southern Sector Rising a few months later as an ad

404. Evelyn Mayo et al., *In Plain Sight: Industrial Compliance Issues in Southern Dallas* (Dallas: Legal Aid of Northwest Texas, 2019).

405. "Stand with Marsha. Move the Mountain.," Southern Sector Rising, accessed February 15, 2021.

406. Robert Wilonsky, ibid.

407. An entire book could and should be written on the environmental racism in Dallas, the list of injustices in South and West Dallas: Shingle Mountain, Lane Plating, Deepwood Dump, Cement City, RSR Lead Smelter, Sand Branch, TX… and the list goes on. For more information on Environmental Justice, see work by Dr. Robert D. Bullard.

hoc coalition to stand up against racist zoning practices in South Dallas.[408]

The *Dallas Morning News* finally began reporting on Shingle Mountain that same month—almost a year after Blue Star began operating. The day after the news broke, the City of Dallas sued Blue Star Recycling, for the first time calling it "large-scale illegal dumping."[409] Blue Star shut down temporarily again but was eventually allowed to start operating as it came back into compliance. Five months into its investigation, the TCEQ initiated enforcement action on Blue Star in early March 2019, placing further scrutiny on the operation from a state level. The state permit showed Blue Star only agreed to store 280 tons of combustible waste for no longer than a week. At that time Blue Star had sixty thousand tons of waste, much of it more than a year old.[410]

Marsha and Southern Sector Rising scheduled a press conference for March 20, 2019, in the Flag Room at City Hall.[411] Just two hours before the press conference, the City pulled Blue Star's certificate of occupancy. When Marsha heard the news,

> "I cried out of relief that something serious was finally being done about a company that's made life miserable for families on our small southern Dallas street for over a year. But I also cried out of anger. This official relief was months in coming and came only because

408. "Outstanding New Activist Organization: Southern Sector Rising," Dallas Peace & Justice Center, accessed February 15, 2021.

409. Robert Wilonsky, ibid.

410. *Downwinders at Risk*, "Toxic Shingle Mountain: Blue Star Recycling's Environmental Crisis in South Dallas," March 19, 2019, video, 4:45.

411. Robert Wilonsky, "Shingle Mountain Fight Came to City Hall," *Dallas Morning News*, March 20, 2019.

I found allies outside my neighborhood to help me fight the shingle storage and grinding operation that resulted in a pile of shingles so large it became visible from nearby highways—allies who were with me at city hall holding a news conference challenging the city's inaction when we got the news."[412]

Marsha raises one of the most important pieces of community action: raising broad based support for the vision through strong allies.

Two days after the press conference at City Hall, Judge Gena Slaughter put a temporary hold on Blue Star's operations.[413] The remainder of the next year played out like a TV drama:

2019

- <u>April 3</u>—Shingle Mountain officially closes and is given a ninety-day notice to remove shingles.
- <u>May 8</u>—Blue Star is unable to pay its lawyer.
- <u>May 24</u>—TCEQ issues $14,000 worth of administrative penalties to Blue Star.
- <u>June</u>—Blue Star CEO Chris Ganter resigns and is replaced by Carl Orrell. Blue Star indicates it does not have the money to clear the property.
- <u>July 2</u>—Blue Star begins trucking shingles out before the ninety-day cleanup expires, attempting to show that work is being done. Judge Slaughter allows an additional 120 days, believing Blue Star is making a "good-faith effort" to clean up the shingles.

---

412. Marsha Jackson, "Every Level of Government Failed Southern Dallas," *Dallas Morning News*, April 2, 2019.

413. Robert Wilonsky, ibid.

- July 4—Steel doors on the Blue Star facility are painted with graffiti: "Warning: Being Black or Brown in Dallas is Hazardous to Your Health" and "Stop Racist Zoning!"
- August 8—Dallas County passes a resolution that blames the TCEQ for allowing Shingle Mountain to exist.
- September 6—Blue Star CEO Carl Orrell resigns, with no suggested replacement.
- October 11—Dallas Mayor Eric Johnson creates a committee to address environmental issues in Dallas (Mayor Johnson still has yet to name Shingle Mountain in public).
- October 17—Evelyn Mayo and Legal Aid of Northwest publish a report titled "In Plain Sight," which outlines the city's zoning failures that allowed Shingle Mountain to occur.
- October 31—Blue Star files for bankruptcy.
- November 22—Former Blue Star leadership is held in contempt of court for not appearing in court or responding to the court's communications.

2020
- February 13—City of Dallas lawyers turn to the owner of the land beneath Shingle Mountain, CCR, to pay for cleanup.
- March 11—Texas Attorney General's office file a petition for the cleanup to finish by mid-June.
- March 12—Trucks arrive at Shingle Mountain briefly beginning to move shingles to another location outside of Dallas.[414]

---

414. Carrington Tatum, "What You Need to Know about Shingle Mountain's Complex History in Southern Dallas," *Dallas Morning News*, September 17, 2020.

After a year of finger-pointing between city, state, and business leaders, Southern Sector Rising began putting additional pressure on city officials. The coalition attempted to get action on the removal of Shingle Mountain from local officials. In mid-2020, another report was released by Evelyn Mayo and students at Paul Quinn College that highlighted and brought more light to air quality issues in South Dallas, including Shingle Mountain and concrete batch plants. Marsha filed a civil suit against the City of Dallas and all parties involved with the site.

By this point, the coalition that stood with Marsha and Southern Sector Rising grew into a group containing faith leaders, nonprofits, advocacy groups, and concerned citizens across the city. Community power continued to energize. In August, "947 days since Marsha Jackson and her Choate Street neighbors awoke… to find their Southern Dallas home surrounded by an illegal dump full of hazardous asphalt shingles," an October 1 ultimatum was given to the City of Dallas to take action on cleaning up Shingle Mountain.[415]

At this point, the group had exhausted all formal pleas to the City and knew that their tactics needed to change.[416] In the wake of George Floyd's murder, the world chanted, "We can't breathe!" in solidarity with Floyd's last words. The same "We can't breathe!" cry echoed through South Dallas.

The shared pain of a racist system, which took George Floyd's breath and life, is taking the breath and life of residents in South Dallas.

---

415. "Stand with Marsha. Move the Mountain.," Southern Sector Rising, accessed February 15, 2021.

416. Carrington Tatum, "In Mock Trials, Protesters Find Dallas Officials Guilty of 'Monstrous Neglect' over Shingle Mountain," *Dallas Morning News*, August 29, 2020.

Members of the coalition built a parade-float-style trailer with an eight-foot-tall Shingle Mountain replica and dragged it around Dallas; they held mock trials in front of city official's homes. When appropriately situated in front of official's homes, members of the twenty-car convoy held mock trials of the officials, playing the theme song from *Law & Order* to commence each trial. All defendants from Mayor Johnson to Judge Slaughter were found guilty of "monstrous neglect." Actor and Downwinders at Risk board member Misti O'Quinn said, "I don't understand what they're waiting for... every day they continue to wait, Marsha gets sicker and sicker."[417]

Lived Experience

Some of the White neighbors interviewed about the protests stated that they disapproved of "the way the protesters went about it." I'd like to take a moment to highlight what I hear in that statement, as a fellow White person: someone is upset that this issue was brought to their doorstep, far removed from the environmental hazard.

It's possible (probable) I'm projecting my own viewpoint onto this analysis. However, when those who are not living with environmental hazards next to their homes turn their nose up about "the way something is done," we are failing to take into account how the system of appeals favors those with White skin and privilege. Shingle Mountain never would have had a living chance to exist in predominantly White North Dallas. White neighborhoods generally aren't surrounded

---

417. Ibid.

with environmental hazards—mine is not—and they allow us to walk outside without the need to make regular visits to a pulmonologist. I think Misti O'Quinn hits the nail on the head: every day of waiting to "do things the right way" is another day our *neighbors* get sicker. As Rabbi Nancy Casten of Temple Emanu-El and Faith Forward Dallas put it, "Just because the residents of Choate Road have survived this abuse for almost three years does not mean it's not an emergency."[418]

Ask yourself: How would you feel if an illegal dump was built outside your bedroom? What if no one heard you complain about it for years while you and your neighbors became more and more sick?

Evelyn Mayo gave some insight into how much work went into getting rid of Shingle Mountain. "At peak moments, [Southern Sector Rising] would meet three times a week, every week, for about eight months," and at a bigger picture, "[It] was two and a half years of nonstop [advocacy work]… there was not a week that went by that we didn't have… an escalation strategy… [we did] everything you can imagine happened to make this go away." It took intense, committed action by the neighborhood and organizers to see action.

Moving Shingle Mountain

What shows up in a week can take infinitely longer to remove.

The work paid off, and the protests were effective. The City of Dallas put out a request for bids to remove Shingle

---

418. Brooklynn Cooper, "Dallas City Council Approves $450,000 Bid to Clean up Shingle Mountain," *Dallas Morning News*, October 13, 2020.

Mountain less than two weeks after the front yard protests.[419] An estimated $2 million cleanup began in mid-December 2020, nearly three years after shingles started showing up outside of Marsha Jackson's bedroom in January 2018.

Every day for almost two months, hundreds of truckloads a day moved the nearly 140,000-ton hazard down the road to McCommas Bluff Landfill, where the shingles would have gone in the first place.[420]

Marsha's coalition finally saw measurable action in service of their community vision. When you're fighting for your community and your life, what other choice do you have but to keep fighting?

Marsha and Southern Sector Rising shared their vision of what they did *not* see for the Floral Farms neighborhood, and the message garnered steady, wide-ranging support across Dallas. The message carried an unfortunately classic power struggle: a small Black and Latinx neighborhood organization facing a (literal) towering threat stood up against a multimillion-dollar business venture run by White men living miles away. As Southern Sector Rising continued to raise support and pressure, they did not let up on the work; Marsha and her allies *fought like hell* to save the vision of their community—perhaps proving once and for all that there is strength in numbers.

———

419. Kevin Krause and Carrington Tatum, "City of Dallas Seeks Contractor to Clean up Shingle Mountain," *Dallas Morning News*, September 10, 2020.

420. "Former Blue Star Recycling Cleanup," City of Dallas, accessed February 18, 2021.

Using Tools to Fight Tools

If you've never sat in on a city council or local government meeting, I can tell you they are filled with jargon and reference codes few people read. Honestly, they are pretty boring. Even for someone who deals in the language of city planning and infrastructure on a daily basis, these meetings can be a lot.

I recently sat in on a Dallas City Plan Commission meeting, and listening to case after case made me realize just how long the city planning process takes (often years), and how specialized some of the knowledge is (i.e., is this land zoned for *light industrial*, *industrial research*, or *industrial manufacturing?*). I also realized city meetings are where the fight for a city's physical future are won or lost, and if residents aren't ready or show up in enough force, it's difficult to influence an otherwise developer driven process like Dallas has. It's easy to see how a disaster like Shingle Mountain can start with a small, seemingly harmless decision in one of these meetings.

I asked Marsha what she thought the most important factors were for fighting racist zoning and environmental racism, and she didn't hesitate to emphasize how crucial a role education plays in community organizing. Education matters for not only understanding an event that will occur, but also its consequences. Thankfully, there are committed groups of people working to eradicate racist zoning practices for future generations.

Jennifer Rangel grew up in Oak Cliff, a primarily Latinx neighborhood south and west of downtown Dallas, west of I-35 from Tenth Street. After graduating from Texas A&M with a major in recreation, park and tourism sciences and minor in urban planning, she set off for the University of North Carolina to get her masters in urban planning. During the December before her graduation, she abruptly changed the topic of her thesis because she "felt the need to do something related to the people in [her] community," ultimately landing on the subject of Latino Urbanism.[421] As is often the case in teaching design, marginalized design theories like Latino Urbanism are often not taught in the classroom, or are only brought up at the end of the lecture as an "Oh, by the way, this also happened..." half-hearted mention. Thankfully, Rangel was willing to dig for the information.

"Within the field of Latino urbanism, people often look at the design and the landscapes, but I wanted to do something different... I wanted to have people tell me how they perceive their environment," Rangel said in an interview, "so it wasn't so much my observations but interviewing [residents and business owners] and learning how they make sense of their surroundings."[422]

Rangel heard stories in her interviews from Oak Cliff residents who had *ganas*: "... They have a willingness to keep pushing forward, but they have lack of access to capital and information."[423] Many residents saw changes in Oak Cliff and grew concerned about whether or not they would have a place there in the future. She heard "a disconnect between [resident's] struggles, and the professionals who are able to help them."[424] One of the central themes Rangel discovered in her master's thesis was the need for informing and

421. Jennifer Rangel, "Neighborhood Equity and Latino Urbanism in Dallas, TX," interview by Demetria McCain, *Inclusive Communities Project*, Storycorp, June 15, 2018, audio, 31:22.

422. Ibid.

423. Ibid. Amanda Merck, "Jennifer Rangel: Creating Bilingual Cartoons to Teach Zoning 101," Salud America!, December 12, 2020.

424. Rangel, ibid.

engaging residents, which is exactly what she has done since she graduated.[425]

Many City of Dallas forms and applications are not translated in Spanish.[426] This creates a tension between residents' struggles and access to information. These language barriers are engagement barriers as well, especially in Dallas, where over 40 percent of residents identify as Hispanic or Latino and nearly the same percentage report speaking Spanish.[427] Through the Inclusive Communities Project, Rangel developed animated videos in English and Spanish to explain what zoning is in simple terms, how it changes, and how people can speak up in the process. Along with a bilingual guide, these resources provide access to information that communities otherwise would have depended on outsiders to translate or provide. Rangel created a permanent resource that provides tools for Spanish speaking residents to understand, engage with, and advocate for their local zoning processes.

———

Planning by the People for the People

Understanding the zoning process is one piece. Engaging the process is another.

As the neighborhoods covered in this book show, power can be leveraged in several ways for positive and negative

425. Jennifer Rangel, "Geographical Examination of Latino Urbanism: Oak Cliff as a Case Study," (master's thesis, UNC Chapel Hill, 2018), 36-44.
426. City Codes now have the option to "translate" on the hosting website.
427. "QuickFacts: Dallas City, Texas," U.S. Census Bureau, accessed January 30, 2021. "Data USA: Dallas, TX," Data USA, accessed March 18, 2021.

interests within planning processes. Whether the interest is obtaining a historical designation for a neighborhood/building or obtaining spot zoning changes to create a new development, land use planning shapes and protects the interest of the city. Which interests are represented is the crucial piece this book is concerned with.

While the fight to move Shingle Mountain was playing out, Jennifer and Evelyn began working with Marsha and the residents of Floral Farms in 2019 to rectify land use issues in the neighborhood. They sought to fight the root cause of why a place like Shingle Mountain existed in their neighborhood in the first place.

"In April or May of that year (2019), while Shingle Mountain was still operating...[a concrete batch plant was] brought to the City Plan Commission to be sited in the neighborhood," Evelyn said. This led the Inclusive Communities Project, Downwinders at Risk, and Southern Sector Rising to speak up. Evelyn said the coalition knew "[we were] just going to continue playing whack a mole if we [didn't] do something about the zoning, because clearly that's what is making this community have a target on [their] back. It's easy land, primed for... terrible uses." After a year of working and building trust with the neighborhood on Shingle Mountain, the coalition received agreement from residents to develop a plan proposing new zoning in line with their vision.[428]

Through the Southern Dallas Neighborhood Defense Project, Evelyn and Jennifer, along with two additional urban planners/activists, Desiree Powell and Emily Fitzgerald, assisted "neighborhood organizations to create and adopt grassroots plans [which express] the desires of residents for

---

428. Jennifer Rangel, "Geographical Examination of Latino Urbanism," 36-44.

their own communities."[429] Think of these grassroots plans as in-depth vision boards saying, "Dear City, here is how land in our neighborhood is currently zoned, here is how it is actually used, here is the vision we see for our neighborhood and what zoning would need to change, and here is how the changes fit within the City's broader goals." Jennifer Rangel emphasizes "the project is a grassroots [planning] approach informed by the community, we are only facilitators."

Floral Farm's neighborhood plan details changes for every nook and cranny of their neighborhood, dividing the neighborhood into subdistricts focused on:

- Community recreation and green space
- Commercial agriculture and residential (feed stores, green houses, etc.)
- Residential agricultural (farm stands, home businesses, etc.)
- Commercial economic development (providing retail goods and services)[430]

Every single one of these subdistricts serves the vision Floral Farms has for themselves: "to preserve the agricultural, single family lifestyle of the community and prevent hazardous industrial encroachment…"[431]

In late 2020, the City of Dallas began the process of evaluating its comprehensive land use plan, ForwardDallas!,

429. "Home," Southern Dallas Neighborhood Self Defense Project, accessed January 30, 2021.

430. *Floral Farms Neighborhood Plan* (Dallas, TX: Neighbors United/Vecinos Unidos & Southern Dallas Neighborhood Self Defense Project, 2020), 33-42.

431. "Floral Farms," Southern Dallas Neighborhood Self Defense Project, accessed February 19, 2021.

originally adopted in 2006. With a strong focus on "promot[ing] equity, economic vitality, and environmental sustainability," the City of Dallas hopes to begin righting past wrongs, many of which we've covered in this book, and many more not covered.[432] Neighborhoods who register plans with the City have an advantage in protecting their visions in planning processes down the road and ideally preventing Shingle Mountains and toxic air pollution from growing in other neighborhoods.

The ability for neighborhoods to build grassroots coalitions and communicate their plans will make significant progress toward greater equity in the future. Jennifer's message to neighborhoods is, "Speak up, make your voice heard, and don't let others decide in your absence what the future of your neighborhood will be."[433]

---

432. "ForwardDallas Comprehensive Land Use Plan Update—About," City of Dallas, accessed January 30, 2021.

433. Jennifer Rangel, "Question Your Surroundings," *Visible Magazine*, May 8, 2019.

11

THE "G" WORD

———

Gentrification is a sticky subject.

Say you've lived in a single family neighborhood for your entire life, and your family home has been passed down through several generations. Recently, new shopping centers and condos have started popping up—you can see them above the roof line of your neighborhood. This is exciting because there are new amenities coming to the community, but the new places are expensive and you can't afford to eat at any of the restaurants or shop at any of the stores. Your annual property tax assessment comes in and your home is assessed against the new buildings down the road. The new appraisals are two to three times as much money as your house was worth just a couple of years ago. In the past seven years your tax bill rose from $300 to $5,500—a nearly $400-per-month increase.[434]

What do you do?

---

434. Keri Mitchell, "Does the Fate of West Dallas Rest on a 400-Foot Tower Next to la Bajada?," *Dallas Free Press*, December 16, 2020.

Do you sell? Do you work another job to pay the taxes? Do you hold out, hoping the price will eventually be high enough you can afford to move somewhere else without a mortgage?

These are questions that families experiencing gentrification are forced to reckon with on a daily basis across the United States.

The previous example is based on present-day experiences in West Dallas's Mexican-American *La Bajada* neighborhood, tucked into the west side of the Trinity River, across the new Margaret Hunt Hill bridge. Many Dallas residents may only know the area by the new name *Trinity Groves*.

Since the early 2000s, a commercial/retail developer bought up a significant portion of land along Singleton Boulevard, where the bridge crosses the Trinity along the southern border of *La Bajada*. It started as a land speculation opportunity buying up what the developers saw as "bottom of the barrel" land.[435] Singleton is now a hotbed of new commercial and retail development, leaving residents concerned if the future of West Dallas includes them.

Half the Battle Is Knowing What to Look For

Discussing gentrification can put up a brick wall in conversations quicker than a new development. Heated debates spring up as people attempt to advocate for either economic development or preventing the displacement of residents (This line

---

435. Peter Simek, "Trinity Groves: The New Dallas Starts Here," *D Magazine*, January 2013.

of thinking assumes the two are mutually exclusive… I argue that they are not). You might even have a general idea of what gentrification looks like: shiny, modern buildings with lots of glass, steel, and brick; clean square lines, exposed ceilings, unfinished floors, economic development, and an influx of new residents. There are preconceived notions about what gentrification removes from a neighborhood as well: crime, poverty, filth, poor infrastructure, and more.

There is little agreement on how gentrification is defined. However, the most widely accepted definition comes from a study authored by the University of Texas in 2018. It defines gentrification with three factors:

1. Displacement of lower income residents
2. Physical transformation of the neighborhood—mostly through the upgrading of housing stock and commercial spaces
3. Changing cultural character of the neighborhood[436]

Displacement is one area many agree is "a matter of concern." It also comes in different forms, making it more difficult to combat. *Displacement* can occur directly through residents' inability to pay bills or are otherwise forced out (through eminent domain, deterioration, etc.). *Indirect displacement* can occur when residents moving out of low-income housing are no longer able to move into other low-income households in the area, indirectly forcing residents out of the neighborhood. Gentrification and displacement are often seen as

---

436. Heather Way, Elizabeth Muller, and Jake Wegman, *Uprooted: Residential Displacement in Austin's Gentrifying Neighborhoods and What Can Be Done about It* (Austin, TX: University of Texas at Austin Center for Sustainable Development, 2018), 15.

directly linked; they force residents out of communities in the name of "improvement."[437]

Identifying those at risk in an area that faces gentrification is crucial. Often, this is referred to as identifying *vulnerable residents*, or those who "are the least able to absorb rising housing costs and whose housing choices are especially limited in the wake of displacement."[438] In the example at the beginning of this chapter, this would be equivalent to selling or moving out of your family home without being able to afford a new place to live. This creates issues around not only housing but employment and other indirect effects of gentrification. Sample vulnerability indicators include:

- Incomes lower than the poverty line
- Communities of color with low household wealth
- Low rates of college-educated residents (who are less likely to be employed in high-earning jobs)[439]

When outside development begins and existing residents in a gentrifying neighborhood are displaced, there is usually less opportunity for existing residents to stay—or return—and take part in the community improvement. This has long been a justified rally cry for grassroots organizers and advocates (present company included) working to fight against the threat of neighborhood displacement.

---

437. Ibid., 16.
438. Ibid., 19.
439. Ibid., 19-22.

The Philadelphia Fed Weighs In

Complicating the matter of displacement, the Philadelphia Federal Reserve Bank issued a report in 2019 suggesting some gentrification-induced displacement may not be as severe as once believed.

The report is co-authored by Quentin Brummet of the University of Chicago and Davin Reed of the Federal Reserve Bank of Philadelphia. Their research pushes against the strong traditional consensus around the negative effects of gentrification on existing residents of neighborhoods experiencing it. In the report, gentrification is strictly defined "as an increase in college-educated individuals' demand for housing in initially low-income, central city neighborhoods."[440] Data in the study covers the one hundred largest metropolitan areas by population (i.e. Dallas, Washington, DC, Charleston, Atlanta, New York, Los Angeles, etc.) from the 2000 census and the 2010-2014 American Community survey.[441] Unlike previous gentrification studies, Brummet and Reed followed up with individual responses over the course of that fourteen years, essentially allowing the study to identify original residents and track their movement over time.[442]

Reed and Brummet found "neighborhoods are far more dynamic than typically assumed."[443] Standard neighborhood to neighborhood migration, without gentrification, was estimated to be 70-80 percent for renters and 40 percent for

440. U.S. Federal Reserve, Federal Reserve Bank of Philadelphia, *The Effects of Gentrification on the Well-Being and Opportunity of Original Resident Adults and Children*, by Quentin Brummet, and Davin Reed, (Philadelphia, Pennsylvania, 2019), 9.

441. U.S. Federal Reserve, *The Effects of Gentrification*, 6.

442. Ibid.

443. Ibid., 4.

homeowners. Meaning, 70-80 percent of the residents in a neighborhood moved between neighborhoods for reasons other than gentrification related causes. The research found gentrification caused 4-6 percent of original residents with less than a college education to be displaced to another neighborhood.[444] At first glance, this feels lower than I wanted to believe. Gentrification *feels* more significant than just 4-6 percent.

Reed and Brummet are able to show that benefits exist for adults and children who can afford to stay in the neighborhoods. There's less exposure to poverty, and some evidence that children are more likely to attend college.[445] This is good news. These are the kinds of benefits Toni Griffin and others advocate for in their work: residents staying in place and benefitting from the positive aspects of gentrification. The authors also acknowledge there are unequally distributed benefits like "higher salaries, better job opportunities, [and] shorter commutes."[446]

Advocates for constructing fair and equitable housing are glad the data confirms there is displacement of residents due to gentrification. However, there remain questions about any disproportionate racial effects, especially for those populations identified as most vulnerable.

———

444. Ibid., 3, 17.
445. Ibid.
446. Peter Simek, "New Study Shows Gentrification May Not Be the Boogeyman Many Fear," *D Magazine*, July 19, 2019.

Real People, Real Outcomes

Psychological effects are also a concern when a neighborhood is gentrified. "Communities perceive it as a violent process," says Karen Chapple of the Center for Community Innovation/Urban Displacement project at UC Berkeley, "and for some it begins a downward spiral."[447]

I agree that Brummet and Reed's definition does not include broader effects of gentrification. By narrowly focusing on the effects of college-educated individuals, the analysis leaves out the potential effects of gentrification largely driven by an increase in outside capital.

Gentrification's perception as a violent process is something that **cannot be overlooked, misunderstood, or written off**. Lived experience is not a data point that can be tossed out because it is harder to quantify. Lived experience is the *lives of neighbors in our cities.*

I cannot stress this enough.

———

Gentrification as Healing: Ogbu's Take

"Why is it that we treat culture erasure and economic displacement as inevitable? We could approach development with an acknowledgment of past injustices—find value not

———

447. Jared Brey, "Study Suggests Gentrification Has an Upside. Housing Advocates Aren't Yet Convinced," Next City, July 25, 2019.

only in those new stories but the old ones, too."[448] Liz Ogbu's construction of justice centers around storytelling.

Growing up in a family of social scientists, Ogbu often refers to herself as the "weird child who drew." Obgu's upbringing also fundamentally shaped the way she viewed the world. Much like my own dinner table conversations impacted the way I thought about the world, the same was true for her. She remembers how her dinner table conversations were filled with "stories of how people lived and connected to one another, from the impact of urban migration on a village in Zambia, to the complex health care needs of the homeless in the streets of San Francisco."[449] Naturally, this spills out into her design practice, Studio O.

On stage at TEDWomen 2017 in New Orleans, LA, Liz told the story of Bayview Hunters Point in Oakland, a site the size of thirty football fields, which for decades contained a Pacific Gas & Electric power plant. Successful lobbying from a mothers group in a nearby public housing development catalyzed the decommissioning and removal of the plant from the community, leaving large swaths of asphalt in its place. Pacific Gas & Electric made an attempt to utilize the space for temporary community organizing, hoping to prevent any negative effects from the abandoned site spilling into the community.[450]

Ogbu brought the asphalt lot to life with events and other community functions, allowing for greater occupation of the space overall. According to Ogbu, nearly twelve thousand

448. Liz Ogbu, "What If Gentrification Was about Healing Communities Rather Than Displacing Them?," filmed November 2017 at TEDWomen, New Orleans, LA, video, 14:54.

449. Ibid.

450. Ibid.

people participated in an event at the former power plant site over a four-year period. This strategy worked until the land was given the green light to develop and talks of redevelopment began.[451]

Liz began to realize "events are not enough." This notion became increasingly evident at one of the community meetings discussing the redevelopment, which she described as "kind of a disaster." During the meeting, decades' worth of pain, suffering, environmental injustice, waste, and economic disenfranchisement bubbled to the surface all at once. The result was cries of a community that fought hard for themselves and the place they called home and faced the fear of gentrification, which history had shown them they would not likely benefit from.[452]

Liz asks us to imagine that our favorite local spot has disappeared, and when we returned home, found out that our rent had doubled; a jarring experience, to be sure. This is the feeling of many people experiencing the effects of gentrification in their neighborhood. It's a pain, Liz says, that "would be the same regardless of whether or not the person who harmed you meant to do so."[453]

What Liz is proposing is a radically different conception of gentrification: gentrification that holds space for pain and acknowledges past injustices. In the search for new possibilities, we leave a trail of "broken promises and squelched dreams." Liz emphasizes, "We are building on top of brokenness. Is it any wonder the foundations cannot hold?"[454]

---

451. Ibid.
452. Ibid.
453. Ibid.
454. Ibid.

Storytelling becomes the mortar for the cracks in the foundation. Liz created space for that pain to be voiced early on in their process. She and her team heard stories from longtime residents lamenting the changes occurring over the years and how the neighborhood was negatively viewed from the outside. From this space, they partnered with StoryCorps to build a listening booth out of a repurposed shipping container. The container created an opportunity for the stories and memories of the place to come alive. As Liz notes, this was still not enough to prevent the surfacing of pain at the community meeting four years later. What it was able to create was a "seed of what [they] did over the next four years."[455]

Pain wasn't erased—that's not the goal of healing. People were listened to, and stories were shared. Instead of offering solutions, Liz offered a path forward, one that creates space for listening to everyone in a city. She adds that listening is "not just about what [we] hope to see built in the future but also about what has been lost or unfulfilled." Even if the path is paved over with thirty acres of asphalt, a highway, or a brand-new condo, the pain remains.

I carry the stories and voices in the first section of this book with me as a reminder to myself that while the physical landscape of Dallas may have changed, the stories continue to live on. It's not a solution to the effects of displacement or gentrification shaping some of the areas now, but, hopefully, it's a step toward healing in the cracks of our city's foundation.[456]

---

455. Ibid.
456. Ibid.

Bringing It Home

The Philadelphia Fed report ranks Dallas as the fifth most populous city in the study and showed a gentrification rate of only 5.9 percent of neighborhoods, placing Dallas as the forty-eighth most gentrifying city of those selected.[457] I'm still unsure what to do with that information. As policy analyst Sarah Treuhaft noted, "We cannot think of gentrification as good when we know it leads to increased displacement of lower-wealth residents and the erosion of cultural diversity and vitality."[458] I agree with her, wholeheartedly. If anything, the report forced me to take a hard look at my own perceptions of gentrification and pull my finger-pointing back ever so slightly.

If some of the effects of gentrification are not as severe as was once believed, how do we handle the reported 4-6 percent of people displaced from their neighborhood due to gentrification? For the City of Dallas, with a population of 1.3 million, and 5.9 percent of neighborhoods "gentrifying," we come out to a back of the napkin estimate of 3,000-4,600 people, roughly the same amount of Dallas residents currently unhoused.[459] That is not an insignificant number, and no individual displaced is insignificant.

Such a complicated process requires a careful contemplation of both empirical and lived experience data to help inform advocacy and policy solutions. If we are to move

---

457. U.S. Federal Reserve, *The Effects of Gentrification*, 40.

458. Brey, ibid.

459. U.S. Federal Reserve, *The Effects of Gentrification*, 40. Metro Dallas Homeless Alliance, *2020 Dallas and Collin Counties Point in Time Homeless Count Results—Summary* (Dallas, TX: Metro Dallas Homeless Alliance, 2020).

forward in redesigning toward ensuring existing residents can afford to stay or move to gentrifying neighborhoods in the future, it will require honest conversations about what that looks like and how it might look different from our traditional conceptions of development.

Planner and activist Desiree Powell summed up Ogbu's concept for me in this way:

> "[Dallas] is… going through the biggest identity crisis, as far as its luxurious condos, downtown, Deep Ellum, Bishop Arts… Oak Lawn. And it seems so progressive on the outside and everyone wants to come here, but when you start unpacking places like Fair Park, Oak Cliff, West Dallas, Vickery [Meadows]… we're the ultimate catfish just for the fact that we bring people here and they have no idea what they're getting into… we've completely… erased the trauma or haven't gone to therapy for it, but we've created this new identity of 'Oh, those things didn't happen…'"[460]

Creating cities/identities that do not bear witness to the trauma of the past and present create a thin façade over a sick heart on the verge of stroke. We continue to build, putting pressure on a broken system, and pushing it to the brink. Stemming further deterioration isn't an issue of bringing in new buildings, it's heart work. Breathing life into our cities will require removing plaque (racism) piece by piece until the blood can flow freely again.

---

460. Catfishing is an attempt to deceive someone by creating a false personal profile online.

12

REINVESTING IN DEVELOPMENT

———

Building a home, business, or large commercial development requires money, and lots of it. Very few people have
the resources to fund their business or development ventures out of pocket, so many people choose to take on loans.
Access to financial capital, like loans, can make or break
a dream. WFAA, a local Dallas news station, conducted a
study in 2020 covering bank lending practices in Dallas
County.[461] The study found that I-30, the generally accepted
border between North and South Dallas, is a dividing line
for lending practices.

Enacted in 1977, the Community Reinvestment Act (CRA)
intended to end discriminatory redlining lending practices
from the Home Owners Loan Corporation and the Federal
Housing Administration dating back at least to the 1930s.[462]
The CRA requires banks to develop and do business in self

———

461. David Schechter et al., "They Underestimate What We Can Do," WFAA-TV,
November 22, 2020.

462. Discriminatory lending practices began before this time period, however,
this is the decade the Federal Government sanctioned these practices
through Home Owners Loan Corporation redlining maps.

determined *assessment areas* (service areas), to meet the needs of the community within that area, including low- and moderate-income neighborhoods.[463] Assessment area maps are required to encompass entire counties or cities, and banks are allowed to cut maps at significant barriers, like a highway, as long as the line doesn't illegally discriminate against a certain demographic (low income, minority, etc.).[464] WFAA's study pulled maps covering all 532 bank branches doing business in Dallas County and found that 20 percent of branches excluded at least some of the area in Dallas County south of I-30.

I was equally outraged and unsurprised at these findings.

Some bank service areas included the bordering Denton and Collin Counties twenty or more miles to the north but did not service neighborhoods south of I-30, only a few miles away.[465] Banks are only regulated on discriminatory practices within their assessment areas, not on how the assessment area is drawn. Essentially, this allows banks off the hook for discriminatory lending practices because they aren't discriminating *within* their assessment areas. If this sounds similar to gerrymandering, your suspicions would be correct. Areas outside of the assessment area end up with less access to capital. In the context of Dallas County, predominantly Black, Latinx, and low-income neighborhoods south of I-30 are legally and disproportionately redlined/gerrymandered out of bank service. This is one form of disinvestment.

---

463. "Community Reinvestment Act (CRA)," Board of Governors of the Federal Reserve System, last updated September 28, 2020, accessed February 7, 2021.

464. Schechter et al., "They Underestimate What We Can Do," November 22, 2020.

465. Ibid.

Private lending follows a trend of fear many large developers (shopping centers, high rises, apartment complexes, etc.) have in regard to doing business in South Dallas. Highlighting this fear of investment, the City of Dallas has a history of using tax subsidies to lure large developers to South Dallas. Developers may come, they may not. In July 2016, the City attempted to lure grocery stores to South Dallas, an area widely evidenced to be a food desert, with a $3 million cash incentive. Businesses did not bite. This is a common refrain not only in Dallas, but in other cities and towns across the country. "There isn't enough demand" or "customer theft" are cited as reasons for an unwillingness to do business in South Dallas communities, which are then perceived from the outside as lacking opportunity. It's a view that focuses on the perceived deficits in South Dallas rather than the assets.[466]

For Monte Anderson, Incremental Is a Big Deal

West of I-35E, and south of downtown Dallas's shadow, lie a group of suburbs referred to as the *Best Southwest Communities*. It's a name used to describe the collective Cedar Hill, DeSoto, Duncanville, and Lancaster area. The four cities make up one of the most demographically diverse regions in the Dallas-Fort Worth Metroplex. Real estate developer Monte Anderson calls Duncanville home.

---

466. Robert Wilonsky, "City Hall Offered $3m To Open a Grocery Store," *The Dallas Morning News*, November 30, 2016.

Monte is a Dallas native, who grew up in Oak Cliff in the '70s. This was a time of transition for Oak Cliff as new subdivisions began popping up and "integration" in Dallas schools was beginning.[467] Integration was also seen in changes on Monte's neighborhood street. Anderson recalled in an interview with Jim Schutze for *D Magazine*, "When the first Black family moved on our street, every person on the street put their house up for sale except for my dad... He was one of those guys who said, [Black families are] just like us, and we're staying."[468]

Anderson is responsible for the rehabilitation of historic buildings like the Texas Theatre in the Bishop Arts district and the restoration of the Belmont Hotel in Oak Cliff. However, his primary focus is the southern sector of Dallas: areas of historic under-investment and lack of interest from large developers. For example, Monte currently has a development in the works in a neighborhood with an average income of $11,759, where a third of the population lives beneath the federal poverty level. I imagine few large developers would jump at that opportunity due to the perceived lack of money to be made. This is one of the pitfalls of traditional development models.[469]

Development Models: Traditional vs. Incremental

Traditional development, as I am defining it in the context of this book, follows a top-down, developer-driven approach. For example, a developer may have an idea for a building,

---

467. Dallas Independent School District did not officially desegregate until 2003, the district is still highly segregated by practice rather than policy.
468. Jim Schutze, "One Dallas Developer's Secret: Bigger Isn't Always Better," *D Magazine*, November 2020.
469. Ibid.

shopping center, or neighborhood and bring that idea to the community. Rather than involving the community from the outset and using community feedback to shape the vision for the development, traditional developers propose a solution based on what they see from a distance.

While traditional development models may believe the only way to invest in South Dallas is through the use of subsidies like tax breaks, Anderson believes in another strategy for making the numbers "pencil out."[470] He advocates for communities to develop buildings and businesses on their own terms, to generate wealth through their own for-profit, small builder-developer models.[471] This means the individual or company develops the land and builds the structure, rather than the two entities being separate. By developing communities from within, rather than relying on outside capital and influence, the Incremental Development (IncDev) approach doesn't require millions of dollars to create meaningful impact in neighborhoods.

IncDev is reinventing how development is carried out. The model lowers the barrier to entry for small, local entrepreneurs to strengthen their neighborhoods.[472] This idea might help return to the practice of building towns Anderson describes "like we used to build them, where the butcher, the baker, and the candlestick maker had two or three [housing] units connected to their business."[473]

---

470. Break even.

471. Monte Anderson, "Monte Anderson on Incremental Development," interview by Kevin Shepherd, *Go Cultivate!*, Verdunity, December 21, 2018, audio, 58:08.

472. "Home," Incremental Development Alliance, accessed November 2, 2020.

473. Jeremiah Jensen, "Developer Monte Anderson Wants To Stop the Handouts," *D CEO*, December 2018.

When I first heard of the incremental approach to developing, it made sense to me; I was practicing this type of development without knowing it had a name. My mother and I started a cookie business out of our home when I graduated from college, using equipment we already had on hand. Over several years, we built up business and partnerships through our friends, neighbors, and our church. After the home bakery laws in Texas expanded in 2013, allowing home-based bakeries to sell at farmer's markets, we took the opportunity to expand our business. We woke up every other Saturday from March through December to sell cookies with little more than a folding tent and table. Our presence at the market brought us new opportunities: we sourced ingredients from farmers and other vendors, we eventually received orders from a local restaurant, and we expanded enough to warrant renting commercial kitchen space.

Our ability to grow slowly over time meant we didn't need to invest in a thousand-square-foot bakery space from the get-go, which would require large loans to cover operating costs. Anderson believes this incremental approach is key for neighborhoods to rebuild equity on their own terms.[474]

Large developments typically require tax subsidies, high rents, and significant amounts of capital backing to make economic sense, preventing many small developers and entrepreneurs from getting to the starting line. This is compounded in neighborhoods of color where access to capital is more limited. With the incremental approach, risk is reduced by building smaller, closer-knit buildings. A business owner or developer can occupy office space on the bottom floor and live in or rent the top floors, creating additional housing in

---

474. Monte Anderson, ibid.

the process. A building with multiple uses increases revenue streams for the developer, reduces risk for the development to pay back loans, and increases the city's tax base.

The IncDev approach promotes local ownership through:

- Updating zoning and city codes to recognize value in small-scale development, working with city governments to understand where barriers to entry exist[475]
- Helping burgeoning business owners access financing
- Mentoring entrepreneurs as they pursue ventures that will bring life to their neighborhoods[476]

Building on an Equitable Foundation

The Government Alliance on Race and Equity (GARE) envisions equitable development as a present and future strategy. Equitable development is a framework that ensures low-income and people of color benefit from urban development and economic growth in their neighborhoods. This is achieved through increasing the capacity of neighborhoods to strengthen their communities and determine their own future.[477]

The GARE framework views achieving equitable development through two main goals:

---

475. "Our Work," Incremental Development Alliance, accessed February 6, 2021.

476. Jeremiah Jensen,ibid.

477. Ryan Curren et al., *Equitable Development as a Tool to Advance Racial Equity,* (Chapel Hill, NC: The Local & Regional Government Alliance on Race and Equity, 2015), 1.

1. Building strong communities and people
   - Increase communities of color's capacity for self-determination
   - Anticipate and prevent displacement of vulnerable residents, businesses, and community organizations

2. Great places with equitable access on all fronts
   - Distribute the benefits and burdens of growth equitably
   - Increase opportunities for low-income households of color to live in all neighborhoods[478]

Development frameworks like IncDev and GARE stand in stark contrast to traditional development models by focusing on community power in decision-making. I'm sure I will get pushback from traditional developers, but I ask that we take a moment to consider how traditional development models, typically funded and carried out by White people, served communities of color in the historical Dallas case study. By my own tally, the neighborhoods rarely benefitted from White outside intervention and instead are either gone or at risk of further erasure today. To move forward equitably, I ask that we reflect on the mechanisms that enable that type of development to perpetuate, and what influence and tools we might have to change that power dynamic.

———

478. Ibid., 16-17.

Doing COIR Work with Derek Avery

Derek Avery grew up in Houston's Third Ward, just two minutes south of downtown. The Third Ward is known as "[Houston's] most diverse Black neighborhood and a microcosm of the larger Black Houston community."[479] The neighborhood is home to the University of Houston, Texas Southern University, and several other amenities.

Next door was one of Houston's freedmen's towns, Fourth Ward. In many respects, the story line for Fourth Ward in Houston is almost identical to North Dallas and Uptown: eminent domain land seizure led to building public housing projects in 1942, an elevated portion of I-45 was built in the 1950s, displacing forty thousand residents, and city-driven redevelopment plans in the 1980s turned the ward into what is now called Midtown.[480]

Proper protections for historic landmarks weren't in place for the Fourth Ward until it was too late, and Derek said, "When you don't have a lot of [landmarks], then it's a free for all for a developer to buy up what they want." Derek grew up in Houston's Third Ward and watched as the neighboring "Fourth Ward [was] rebranded [into] Midtown... Just [watching] that whole process was pretty sickening." This experience living in a transitional and underserved neighborhood drives his entire philosophy of development: revitalization *without* gentrification.[481]

---

479. Roger Wood, *Down in Houston: Bayou City Blues,* (Austin, TX: University of Texas Press, 2003), 71.

480. Tomiko Meeks, "Freedman's Town: A Lesson in the Failure of Historic Preservation," *Houston History Magazine* 8 (no. 1, 2011), 44.

481. "Our People," COIR Holdings, accessed November 2, 2020.

Derek's focus is on developing quality homes in neighborhoods within a few miles of a central business district. His starting point in any city is usually Martin Luther King Jr. Boulevard with the expectation that it will be "a Black Mecca of the city where... you see the most thriving Black owned businesses...[and] people investing in that area, particularly Black people." Unfortunately, for many of the reasons discussed in this book, Derek said, "You don't see [the] same type of development in those areas, and that's why I always check... I always want to start at MLK and develop outward."

Derek owns Community Outreach Initiative for Redevelopment (COIR) Holdings and is adamant about not being a "spreadsheet developer," and instead being a "community developer."[482] Derek says, "One of the things I think we forget, is when you look at development on a short-term basis, it's just purely profit-driven. But if you're looking at it from a long-term basis, then it's deeper than just profit—you're actually redeveloping the area when it comes to the people, when it comes to the culture."[483]

COIR shifts away from traditional development approaches by viewing the neighborhood's people and culture as assets.

Derek says the struggle is "you can't have concentrated poverty, but you [also] can't displace everyone."[484] COIR fights displacement through personally offering free property tax consulting for all residents on the street a new home may

482. *Coir is the outside fiber of a coconut and is strong enough to be used as rigging on ships when woven together.* Audrey Byron, "Can You Have Revitalization Without Gentrification?," Strong Towns, October 23, 2018.

483. Derek Avery, "Revitalization Without Gentrification—With Derek Avery," interview by Ryan Short, *Eyes on the Street*, CivicBrand, May 12, 2020, audio, 10:55.

484. Audrey Byron, ibid.

be built on. The emphasis is on protecting residents from tax increases their budgets may not be able to handle, increasing the likelihood they can remain in their homes.

For example, a traditional developer may build a home on a street. The new building will be compared, from a property tax perspective, to a home built one hundred years ago down the street. Derek says "it's apples and oranges." The new home may be appraised at several hundred thousand dollars more than the existing home, leading the existing home to be compared for tax appraisal against this much more expensive home. The result is a higher property tax bill for the existing homeowner. Some developers will file for tax comparisons to be based on the value of the land rather than the value of the home. Unfortunately, this only makes it easier for developers to compare dissimilar properties and still drive up the land appraisal. Again, the result is a higher property tax bill. In either scenario, for a homeowner on a fixed or low income, price increases can end up in displacement.

Context Matters

Needless to say, the COIR approach to development where you're investing in residents who aren't even purchasing homes from you requires a lot of listening and intention. COIR's developments seek to:

> "understand the history first, to understand what's missing, what's causing there to be dis-investment in that neighborhood. From there, we say, 'What product makes sense? What will get rooftops here and get people who used to live here or are form here to move

back?… We want to fill that void of: what do we give them, what is there for them to come back to so that we can weave that community back together and revitalize it back to where it was when it was thriving?"[485]

It's not redevelopment—it's revitalization: breathing life into the bones already in the community.

Historical contextualization is crucial for the success of not only the community but the developers as well. Preservation practices create opportunities for equipping neighborhoods and developers with more information and understanding of a neighborhood. Derek thinks "if you understood the history of the area and educated yourself on [it], you would see it less as a complication and more… honoring this history—I can build around what's already there and build… on scale with [what is existing]." For Derek, history is not an impediment. Historical framing is an opportunity for developers to be more receptive to resident input when approaching a development and respect neighborhood identifiers like neighborhood and street names.[486]

The key aspect for revitalization is ensuring development helps residents build up amenities in their neighborhood, but not at the cost of displacement or erasure of history. Evidence in the first half of this book shows what traditional developers, local governments, and other systems of power have done and continue to do: a terrible job of preventing these

---

485. Derek Avery, and Bianca Avery, "Can You Have Revitalization Without Gentrification? With Bianca & Derek Avery," interview by Jordan Clark, *Go Cultivate!*, Verdunity, March 14, 2019, audio, 34:00.

486. *This is similar to how Uptown and Little Mexico are called Uptown, Oak Lawn, etc., and Houston's Fourth Ward is now called Midtown.* Derek Avery, ibid.

negative outcomes. Equitable development requires what many will consider a radical rethinking of how we approach development and redistribute power in the process back into the hands of our BIPOC neighbors. Derek just asks, "Please don't Uptown my South Dallas."

13

A DIVERSITY OF ACTORS

In my role as a utility engineer, I came into contact with an incredible number of stakeholders working at the municipal, county, and state level in Texas. From searching for landowner and right-of-way information in small West Texas county clerk's offices to being grilled by TXDOT project managers wanting to know when a pipeline relocation would be out of the way of highway construction in Dallas, my work has led to interactions with all sorts of people.

More often than not, my interactions were with people who looked like me: White, male, college graduates. I didn't have to think much as I moved in and around these spaces because my experience was often considered the default. I have found this to be the default for other fields responsible in shaping our cities, including (but not limited to) engineers, urban planners, and architects. In my time as a utility engineer, I only remember one period where I was the minority in my work group, and that experience only lasted five months.

When I transferred from Fort Worth to Dallas, I worked for a young Black man recently promoted to engineering manager. The other members of our engineering team were another White man, a White woman, and another Black man. Our team maintained this relative diversity for a year or so until the other White man took an opportunity to work in another engineering team. When his vacancy was filled, our manager hired a Black man from another gas utility, who coincidentally attended my rival high school. We figure we probably sat across from each other under the Friday night lights at some point in time. Small world.

I was now the lone White male viewpoint within the immediate engineering group.

Whether its makeup was intentional or not, it was the most racially diverse engineering team in the division at that time. Five months later, at the beginning of 2015, I transferred to Lubbock, Texas. Out of the six engineers on that team, five were White men, and our lone female representative identified as Mexican-American. It was back to status quo.

Neither of these teams was inherently better or worse than the other. However, when a dominant viewpoint begins as a smaller trend within a team and organization then ripples out into an industry, there is a greater chance for voices and viewpoints to be left out of the conversation. Without a diversity of actors, we risk a loss of equity in our industries, organizations, and neighborhoods.

The question I keep asking myself is: "How can I as a White man possibly design space intended for Black and Brown experiences?"

The answer is: I cannot do it alone.

———

Diversity in Numbers

Racial diversity is more than a numbers game, even though the numbers are important.

According to a National Science Board analysis in 2020, the engineering field was 61 percent White, 24 percent Asian, 9 percent Hispanic, 4 percent Black, and 0.6 percent combined American Indian or Native Hawaiian.[487]

Census numbers from 2018 show the urban planning field was 80 percent White, 9 percent Asian, 5 percent Black, 2.5 percent Hispanic, and nearly 0 percent for all other demographics.[488]

Similarly, in 2017, the architecture field was estimated at 72 percent White, 11 percent Asian, 4 percent Black, 2.5 percent Hispanic, and nearly 0 percent for all other demographics.[489]

Aside from those identifying as Asian, all racial minority groups are underrepresented in professions shaping our cities compared to their representation in the overall US population. This can make it exceedingly difficult for all viewpoints to be appropriately represented at the drafting table. Valerie Franklin, president of Nashville's chapter of the National Organization of Minority Architects (NOMA), best describes this effect: "Often when someone is not afflicted by something, they have the perception that it does not exist."[490]

Marsha Jackson's experience with Shingle Mountain is a prime example of this. I am sure many readers of this book

---

487. Amy Burke, *Science and Engineering Labor Force* (Alexandria, VA: National Science Board, 2019).
488. "Urban & Regional Planners," Data USA, accessed December 29, 2020.
489. "Architects, Except Naval," Data USA, accessed December 29, 2020.
490. Jessie Taylor, "In Conversation With: Valerie Franklin," Nashville Design Week 2020, accessed December 28, 2020.

have not lived next to an industrial site or landfill. I do not. It is a privilege not to be afflicted by hazardous sites in my neighborhood, which also makes them easy to forget. Writing off Marsha's experience would be very easy if I chose to ignore it. However, I've talked to Marsha and heard the rasp in her voice and the struggle to speak at times. You've now read about it and other instances of injustice here in Dallas, so you're on the hook. How can you get a greater understanding of people in your community with experiences different from your own?

———

Pascale Goes beyond the Built Environment

An architecture professor at the Pratt Institute in Brooklyn told Pascale Sablan she would never become an architect because of her gender and color.[491] She, and others, are proving him wrong.

Sablan is a highly accomplished and awarded architect. She currently serves as the president-elect for NOMA National, holds multiple awards from the American Institute for Architecture, has served on several boards of directors, founded her own advocacy group, lectures across the country, and is a senior associate for S9 Architecture in New York City.

Sablan actively works to change and claim the narratives for all women and designers of color contributing to the built environment.[492] Sablan is only the 315th Black woman in United States history to become a licensed architect (tens of thousands

---

491. Elizabeth Fazzare, "Architect-Advocate Pascale Sablan Is Revising the History of the Built Environment," Forbes, September 26, 2020.
492. Ibid.

of White men are currently licensed architects in the US), a fact that in many ways drives her work and advocacy.

Fifteen to twenty thousand Black enslaved people are buried in lower Manhattan just one block away from City Hall and the Tweed Courthouse.[493] The African Burial Ground National Monument in New York was Sablan's first project to contribute to, sharing the history and narrative of the thousands of Black people responsible for building the nation's largest city who were later built upon.[494]

Sablan's Hatian heritage made her an ideal candidate for a role in rebuilding a school campus destroyed in Haiti's 2010 earthquake.[495] Sablan designed the sprawling, sustainable campus with help from predominantly BIPOC students in an architecture, construction, and engineering mentorship program. Every facet, from the light in the buildings to the flood water collection areas, was designed for the space to serve the students and the surrounding community.[496] The intersection of design and activism for underrepresented communities is the hallmark of Sablan's work.

Sablan founded Beyond the Built Environment (BBE) at the end of 2018, advocating for and engaging equitable, reflectively diverse environments.[497] BBE grew out of a concern she developed when Googling "great architects" and not coming

---

493. "History & Culture," African Burial Ground National Monument, April 26, 2019.

494. "Architect Pascale Sablan Honored With 2021 Whitney M. Yound Jr. Award," American Institute of Architects press release, December 9, 2020 on the American Institute of Architects website, accessed December 27, 2020.

495. Ibid.

496. Ibid. "Architect Pascale Sablan Honored," American Institute of Architects, December 9, 2020. Pascale Sablan, "Redesign a School," (PowerPoint presentation at the Brooklyn Vol. 4 "Brooklyn Vol. 4—Design Week," Brooklyn, NY, May 18, 2015).

497. "Home," Beyond the Built Environment, accessed December 28, 2020.

across anyone looking like her.[498] Out of all the lists popping up, only nine people of color were present.[499] BBE is on a mission to correct that underrepresentation.

The organization leverages Sablan's "Triple E, C" advocacy framework to holistically address inequities in architecture:

- Engage—diverse audiences through programming, promoting intellectual discourse and exchange
- Elevate—identities and contributions of minority architects
- Educate—masses through formal and informal learning opportunities that introduce architecture as a bridge to fill the gaps of inequity
- Collaborate—with community stakeholders and organizations to crowdsource information and amplify opportunities to advocate for equitable and reflectively diverse environments[500]

Since 2018, BBE develops exhibitions highlighting local diverse designers through city-specific programming under the name *Say It Loud*. Sablan says celebrating these designers is harder than you might think; "I spend a lot of time telling people they're worthy of praise and elevation, debunking the misconception that they should be principals (head of an architecture firm) to be celebrated and convincing them to claim their contributions."[501]

---

498. Anjulie Rao, "Stand Up and Stand Out," *Landscape Architect Magazine*, May 2020.

499. Ibid.

500. "Architect Pascale Sablan Honored," American Institute of Architects, December 9, 2020. Pascale Sablan's LinkedIn Profile, accessed December 30, 2020.

501. Rao, ibid.

BBE elevates diverse designers through the Great Diverse Designers Library. Currently, 423 women (of any ethnicity) and BIPOC designers (architects, planners, engineers, scientists, artists, etc.) are recorded in the online platform, "[sharing] their story from their perspective and [curating] their journey as they introduce themselves and their work to society and our global community."[502]

———

See It to Be It

Our day-to-day understandings are built from interactions occurring over the course of our lifetimes. The actions and environments you're exposed to greatly impact your understanding of what may be possible for the world and yourself. Psychologist Albert Bandura describes this phenomenon through the *social cognitive theory* he developed in the 1980s. The theory supports the idea that we learn from observing behaviors in our environments and the observations and responses to those behaviors determine whether those actions should be reinforced or not. Under Bandera's theory, if you aren't exposed to certain behaviors, it is possible a behavior may not be learned or exist within your frame of reference. Essentially, if you can't see it, that makes it difficult to be it.[503]

NOMA seeks to change what youth see as possible for their future. For the most part, the professions discussed in

502. "Great Diverse Designers Library," Beyond the Built Environment, accessed December 31, 2020.
503. Saul, McLeod, "Albert Bandura's Social Learning Theory," *Simply Psychology*, accessed January 15, 2021.

this book are relatively invisible to the community. Mark Ripple, partner at Eskew+Dumez+Ripple, notes youth "have the opportunity to see what [first responders] do, what teachers do, what good chefs do, [but] they don't have the opportunity to see what architecture is about."[504] While the finished product of architect's work is highly visible, the behind-the-scenes work often goes unseen.

Since 2005, NOMA chapters have worked in schools across the country to introduce students to the process of design, the significance of architecture in daily experiences, and its cultural, social, and historic impact on our cities. Summer camps, workshop series, and design competitions are the framework for the pipeline; these practices engage youth while also engaging the architecture community. While the primary participants are students in junior high and high school, instructors are undergraduate college students, young professionals in the industry, or teachers in nearby architecture schools. Each local NOMA chapter creates its own networks and camps meeting its specific context and needs.[505]

————

Diversity of Opinion

Engaging in diversity goes beyond racial diversity in professional disciplines. Professionals are merely one piece of the puzzle in shaping our cities. We often place extensive

---

504. "Project Pipeline." n.d. NOMA Louisiana, accessed December 26, 2020.
505. Ibid.

value on expert opinions while disregarding the value of lived experience to inform the design process.

My utility engineering team came from a variety of engineering disciplines: civil, mechanical, and electrical. While we each held relatively diverse sets of engineering lenses, we generally had a common approach to problem solving and a linear way of thinking about our work.

Through that traditional engineering lens, I viewed projects through the frame of mind as a problem needing fixing. Narrowly defined, my job as an engineer was to fix problems. Engineers are trained to define, understand, and troubleshoot all versions of a problem to find the most efficient solution, however efficiency is defined.

I think there are areas for improvement in my past work. I did my best to work closely with internal and external stakeholders finding common ground and an agreeable solution for all parties. However, my traditional approach to designing a solution was focused on a set of inputs that did not include all impacted parties.

For example, I typically opened up Google Earth and began drawing imaginary lines through cities, dodging buildings, bodies of water, and other potential difficulties. I drew routes that looked clear based on information gathered from the aerial view on a computer screen. This would go through a couple of internal revisions to determine the most likely candidates for construction from a back-of-a-napkin estimate. I laced up my steel toe boots and headed out to walk the proposed locations, gathering more information.

I teamed up with our field personnel and we developed a plan for what would be easiest to construct and cause the least amount of visible disruption. We truly worked to minimize our impact to the surrounding community. However, we were all utility personnel, using utility experience and knowledge to solve a utility problem; it is an analytical framework shaped by more than a century of lessons learned. We did not always involve residents or small businesses in the planning and design phases of our projects. I look back and see how the work I performed followed a common pattern of identifying large entities or customers impacted by the work and not necessarily digging deeper (no pun intended). Today, I would partner more closely with the community to understand the dynamics of the neighborhood. My designs may not change with that information, but I would at least understand the way a project fit within the neighborhood context.

I am seeing how I participated as one of the same agencies with power to control the shape of the city. We were the ones calling the shots. This was a common approach when Central Expressway was built in the 1940s and holds true in the modern-day context. While positive strides have taken place in public engagement since the 1940s, the large proportion of decision-making in our cities lies within the hands of those who build and shape it. If we are seeking to build equitable cities, stakeholder diversity and engagement needs to grow, in the words of Pascale Sablan, beyond the built environment.

Honor the Griot

Professionals of any stripe have a tendency to approach knowledge accumulation through increasingly academic and scholarly methods. I've noticed this in my own graduate work as I am asked to find "reputable" and "scholarly" justification to back up my analysis. I find myself evaluating the validity of a resource based on whether or not it came from an academic journal or not. While I appreciate the need for rigorous study to prove out theories, there is significant benefit to including more informal, and coproduced sources of knowledge in the design process.

I can't even begin to count the number of times people haven't spoken up about one of my designs because I'm an engineer; that people are conditioned to think that engineers are experts that shouldn't be challenged. More often than not, my experience has shown me that engineers working in communities are *not* experts.

Communities are full of experts (with lived experience) who probably think about problems in their neighborhoods more than interloping professionals.

Bryan C. Lee describes the value of this communal expertise through the first two of his eight design justice principles of process: *honor the griot* and *power in place*.[506]

The griot (pronounced GREE-oh) oral history tradition comes from West Africa.[507] History of and information about a community is held through the griot tradition and is communicated by song.[508] The griot serve an important role in helping African communities tell their own stories rather than have their narratives dominated by a White, Western lens.[509]

Griot knowledge is gained from within the community themselves, through self-sustaining channels, rather than knowledge gained through a top-down approach initiated

506. *Columbia GSAPP*, "Bryan C. Lee, Jr. 2020," September 28, 2020, video, 1:32:18.
507. Fran Kaplan, "What Is a Griot?," America's Black Holocaust Museum, accessed December 29, 2020.
508. Ibid.
509. Maya Elese, "Knowledge Session: The Griot Tradition," I Am Hip Hop Magazine, March 18, 2018.

by an outside agent. Lee describes griots as the "Ms. Mary's" on the block:

> "The people who have lived in a particular community for years, and years, and years, and understand where the crack in 1968 happened in the sidewalk on Smith Street. They understand precisely how a neighborhood functions because they've lived there for so long and they can understand its nuances."[510]

Including community griot in the design and knowledge building in a project can fundamentally shift power dynamics in a project.[511] Imagine how you might understand a neighborhood as more than just the sum of the cracks in the sidewalk if you knew how the cracks happened and how long they have existed. Imagine what it feels like when your voice is not included in making a decision that will affect you and your neighbors.

———

Power in Place

Evaluating stakeholder engagement is a crucial step toward challenging existing power structures existing in the built environment and increasing the diversity of actors present in the design process.

510. *Columbia GSAPP,* "Bryan C. Lee, Jr. 2020," September 28, 2020, video.
511. Co-production of knowledge is a balance between the superiority of highly specialized knowledge and the lived experience of grassroots organizing. Diane Archer, and David Dodman, 2015, "Making Capacity Building Critical...," *Urban Climate,* 14 (1): 68-78.

Lee's *power in place* principle focuses more specifically on building collective power to address systemic issues in the built environment.[512] I am borrowing a definition of *power* here: "Being high in power implies having control over relatively more resources, while being low in power implies having relatively less control over valued resources."[513] Our design processes must fundamentally change their structure in order for existing power dynamics to shift.[514]

In my experience, including customer or landowner input earlier in the process usually developed better solutions in the long run. The projects that had the most trouble were ones where landowners felt a lack of agency in the entire process. Sometimes more money isn't the solution to a problem—especially when an existing power dynamic becomes further entrenched in the process.

More often than not, community knowledge is extracted for use in the design process, free of charge, from those who've born down the cost of obtaining the knowledge inherent in lived experience.

Collectively building power in the design process looks different but is not unachievable. Honoring the griot and recognizing the level of knowledge *within* a community requires an abdication of power from design professionals. This means having defined, and paid, seats at the table for those in the

512. *Columbia GSAPP*, "Bryan C. Lee, Jr. 2020," ibid.

513. Michael Schaerer et al.,"Low Power Individuals in Social Power Research: A Quantitative Review, Theoretical Framework, and Empirical Test," *Organizational Behavior and Human Decision Making* 149, (November 2018): 73.

514. Sonia Matera, "The Role of Power Dynamics for Community Engagement: A Case Study in Myanmar," masters thesis, (Sweden: LUND University, 2020).

community providing input into the design process.[515] Literally and figuratively honoring the value of lived community experiences has the potential to embed greater equity in the design process and challenge existing power structures.

Lee writes, "[Power in place] seeks to challenge [these structures] and forward the efforts of racial, social, and cultural reparation through the processes and outcomes of design."[516]

In an interview with *Cultured Magazine*, Pascale brought the fight for justice home. She rightly asserts, "Advocacy work can and should start on your block, in your neighborhood, in your community. See what injustices are impacting your town and take that as a beginning standpoint."[517]

That being said, one chapter on diversity does not cover the range or depth of this issue, let alone one written from the bias of a White male. While I attempt to elevate diverse and underrepresented viewpoints in this book and this chapter, I know this is just the beginning of the real work.

Increased representation in all aspects of designing cities and their infrastructure allows for other experiences and viewpoints to be brought to the table in otherwise White male dominated fields. This is precisely why equity-centered design frameworks call for a diversity of viewpoints and participants. It is more challenging to meet our visions of just cities if a broad range of viewpoints and perspectives are ignored.

We must reinvest in the fields and stakeholders charged with shaping our cities if we want to have any hope of building more equitable cities.

---

515. *Columbia GSAPP*, "Bryan C. Lee, Jr. 2020," September 28, 2020, video. Creative Reaction Lab, *Equity-Centered Community Design Field Guide* (St. Louis, MO: Creative Reaction Lab, 2018).

516. *Columbia GSAPP*, "Bryan C. Lee, Jr. 2020," ibid.

517. Fazzare, ibid.

CONCLUSION

PAVING A NEW WAY

"The only future we deserve is the one we are willing
to work for, fight for, and invest in right now."

—REV. DR. STARSKY WILSON[518]

To say this journey has been life-changing is both a cliché
and an understatement. What started out as an exploration
of highway design led to a fundamental shift in understanding of the place I've called home for nearly thirty-two years.
Dallas was built and is being rebuilt in ways that benefit the
needs and desires of people who look like me. If I don't want
to, I don't have to think critically about Dallas because it was
designed by and for me.

Our built environment is a reflection of what and who we
value. However, at the end of the day, it's about more than
just infrastructure. Infrastructure and the shape of our cities
today are symptomatic of the larger ill—racism—which has

---

518. *Urban Institute,* "Keynote Address from Rev. Starsky Wilson, President
and CEO of Children's Defense Fund," January 19, 2021, video, 18:56.

propped up inequitable systems for centuries. Infrastructure is an expression of what we collectively place the most value on: power and privilege.

As our infrastructure ages, we find ourselves at a time when many of the projects discussed in this book are at a reckoning point. We face decisions with long-term consequences.

I-345, the elevated highway separating Deep Ellum from downtown Dallas, is hanging on for dear life. A team of TxDOT engineers found the design (as an elevated and curving structure, combined with the heavy use) places an enormous amount of stress on the bridge's steel components. Imagine several hundred thousand vehicles going around an elevated curve at high speed, and you can get a feel for what that might do to a bridge over time.

It is hard to imagine life in Dallas without I-345—it has served commuters for decades. TxDOT decided in 2015 the best option at the time was to patch the bridge by welding steel reinforcing plates to the weakening structure, giving it life for another twenty years. Designs are currently underway to replace I-345 with either another bridge, a tunnel, or a series of surface boulevards.

I-345 is not the only highway in Dallas under the microscope—both I-30 and I-35 are currently under construction or review for replacement. We make decisions daily within visible and invisible systems that continue to shape our cities. However, we must ask ourselves *now*, as we attempt to reinforce our infrastructure: will we continue to reinforce racism and similar perpetuated systems of injustice, or do we choose to invest in a new direction?

I am investing in a new direction.

I am paving a new way.

ACKNOWLEDGEMENTS

Thank you to everyone who has helped me bring *Paved A Way* to life, whether you helped me write it or just finished reading it.

This book has been one of the most life-changing projects I've embarked on, and I hope it sparks change in your life as well.

Thank you Mom and Dad for showing me what it looks like to live a life caring about the world and people around me. Watching both of you serve the community and work toward greater equity in the world has formed so much of who I am today. You both have supported me as I stepped away from my corporate job and leaned into this new life, I can't thank you enough for the pep talks and accountability. Also, thank you to all of my siblings, Jennifer, Elizabeth, and David, who encouraged me with my *many* projects over the years and continue encouraging me no matter what!

Lauren, thank you for standing with me as I've journeyed through this project and change in my life. From helping me think through analogies to writing on popsicle sticks for every one hundred words I wrote, you supported me through thick and thin. I am so grateful for you.

Justin Childress, your Context & Impact of Design class fundamentally changed my life. I don't know why you put Central Expressway on a list of Dallas design landmarks, but I am thankful it was there. Thank you for the ability to explore ideas and the initial, possibly joking, encouragement to turn that paper into a book. Jessica Burnham, on multiple occasions you allowed this seminary turned MASD student to crash your program and continued to support my work even when I wasn't one of your own students. Thank you. And Jennifer Ebinger, who brought this book writing program to my attention, thank you for encouraging me, and others, to join and successfully complete this process.

A huge thanks goes to my two principal editors, Quinn Karrenbauer and Kristin Gustafson. Quinn, thank you for helping me break up my academic writing style and help me believe I can write thousands of words. Kristin, thank you for continually walking me back from the brink, advocating for me, and helping me push my writing to a whole new level, centering the voices of the communities in the narrative.

Writing *Paved A Way* has been the journey of a lifetime, and it wouldn't have been possible without the support of the Book Creator's Institute and New Degree Press. Huge thank you to Eric Koester at the BCI, and Brian Bies, Amanda Brown, Kyra Ann Dawkins, Gjorgji Pejkovski, Mackenzie Finklea, and everyone else at NDP. Y'all are amazing.

Finally, a special thank you to the people who preordered *Paved A Way* and supported the book early on:

Abbey A.	Ed F.
Albert V.	Edward E.
Alison W.	Elizabeth C.
Amir G.	Elizabeth M.
Amy S.	Elizabeth S.
Andrew B.	Elizabeth W.
Andy T.	Eric K.
Angela S.	Eric T.
Ann M.	Everett B.
Anna M.	Finn D.
Barbara C.	Gerald S.
Becky W.	Heather R.
Beth E.	Jacob L.
Bob C.	Jacob S.
Carol C.	JC S.
Caroline C.	Jeff H.
Carolyn M.	Jennifer H.
Cassie P.	Jennifer K.
Chris F.	Jennifer R.
David M.	Jesse S.
David D.	Jessica B.
David P	Jessica B.
David Y.	Jessica C.
Deborah C.	Joel S.
Deborah Y.	Juliana M.
Dennis S.	Justin C.
Desiree P.	Kaci M.
Doug H.	Kathleen A.
Ebun O.	Kathleen F.

Kathleen O.

Kelee L.

Kelly M.

Kevin R.

Kirstin C.

Korey F.

Kristin J.

Kyle S.

Laura B.

Lauren Anne C.

Laure D.

Linda I.

Lindsay B.

Marco G.

Marissa N.

Mary Lu H.

Matt H.

Matt M.

Megan O.

Megan W.

Mike E.

Michele B.

Mike D.

Mindy W.

Molly S.

Monica M.

Nick M.

Rachel K.

Rachel M.

Rachel R.

Rhonda W.

Ryan D.

Sandra O.

Sawyer S.

Scott S.

Shannon G.

Steve B.

Steve R.

Steven J.

Steven M.

Steven R.

Steven T.

Tammy E.

Tanya C.

Thada K.

Tim M.

Tina B.

Travis C.

Tyler R.

Vic H.

Wendy W.

William J.

Willie B.

Wilson S.

APPENDIX

Built On Stolen Land

Allison, Wick. "How Dallas Became Big D." *D Magazine*, September 2008. https://www.dmagazine.com/publications/d-magazine/2008/september/how-dallas-became-big-d/.

Anderson, Gary Clayton. *The Conquest of Texas: Ethnic Cleansing in the Promised Land, 1820-1875.* Norman, OK: University of Oklahoma Press, 2005.

Bailey Jr., Everton. "Dallas City Council Approves Renaming Street in Memory of Botham Jean." *Dallas Morning News*, January 13, 2021. https://www.dallasnews.com/news/politics/2021/01/13/dallas-city-council-approves-renaming-street-in-memory-of-botham-jean/.

"American Indians: A Story Told for Thousands of Years," Bullock Museum, accessed November 10, 2020. https://www.thestoryoftexas.com/discover/campfire-stories/native-americans.

Claeys-Shahmiri, Janet. "Ethnohistorical Investigation of the Battle of Village Creek, Tarrant County, Texas, in 1841." (master's thesis,

University of Texas at Arlington, 1989). https://www.proquest.com/dissertations-theses/ethnohistorical-investigation-battle-village/docview/193890381/se-2?accountid=6667.

Dallas Truth, Racial Healing & Transformation. *A New Community Vision for Dallas: 2019 Report.* Dallas, TX: Dallas Truth, Racial Healing & Transformation, 2019. https://dallastrht.org/resources/.

Dallas Truth, Racial Healing & Transformation. "Home." Accessed December 26, 2020. https://dallastrht.org/.

Denton History Information. "The Battle of Village Creek: The Texas Sentinel." Accessed November 10, 2020. http://www.dentonhistory.info/denton/villagecreek/.

Donald S. Frazier, "Battle of Village Creek," Texas State Historical Association Handbook of Texas, accessed November 10, 2020. https://www.tshaonline.org/handbook/entries/village-creek-battle-of.

McElhaney, Jackie, and Michael V. Hazel. "Dallas, TX." Texas State Historical Association Handbook of Texas. Accessed February 21, 2020. https://www.tshaonline.org/handbook/entries/dallas-tx.

Native Governance Center. "A Guide to Indigenous Land Acknowledgment." Accessed February 21, 2021. https://nativegov.org/a-guide-to-indigenous-land-acknowledgment/.

Smith, F. Todd. *The Caddo Indians: Tribes at the Convergence of Empires, 1542-1854.* College Station: Texas A&M University Press, 1995.

Texas Historic Sites Atlas. "Details for Village Creek (Atlas Number 5439005654)." Accessed November 10, 2020. https://atlas.thc.texas.gov/Details/5439005654.

U.S. Department of Arts and Culture. "Honor Native Land: A Guide and Call to Acknowledgment." Accessed February 21, 2021. https://usdac.us/nativeland/.

Whorton, Brenda B., and William L. Young. "Before John Neely Bryan: An Overview of Prehistoric Dallas County." *Legacies: A History Journal for Dallas and North Central Texas*, (3) 2, Fall 1991, 4. https://texashistory.unt.edu/ark:/67531/metapth35119/.

The Central Argument

Barr, Alwyn. *Black Texans: A History of Negroes in Texas, 1528-1971.* Austin: Jenkins Pub. Co., 1973.

City of Dallas Office of Economic Development. "Uptown PID." Accessed October 1, 2020. https://www.dallasecodev.org/493/Uptown-PID.

Dallas Express. "Central Boulevard to Take in Homes of Long-Time Residents," October 5, 1946.

Dallas Morning News. "Central Expressway Readied for Opening," July 28, 1949.

Davidson, James M. "An Archival History of Freedman's Cemetery, Dallas, Texas." In *Freedman's Cemetery: A Legacy of a Pioneer Black Community in Dallas, Texas,* edited by Duane E. Peter, Marsha Prior, Melissa M. Green, and Victoria G. Clow, 21-50. Plano: Geo-Marine, Inc., 2000.

Fairbanks, Robert B. *The War on Slums in the Southwest: Public Housing and Slum Clearance in Texas, Arizona, and New Mexico, 1935-1965.* Philadelphia: Temple University Press, 2014.

Head, Louis P. *The Kessler City Plan for Dallas: A Review of the Plan and Progress on Its Accomplishment.* Dallas: Dallas Morning News, 1925. https://texashistory.unt.edu/ark:/67531/metapth207135/m1/18/.

George Kessler, *A City Plan for Dallas.* Dallas: Dallas Park and Recreation Department, 1911. https://texashistory.unt.edu/ark:/67531/metapth129158/.

Payne, Darwin. *Quest for Justice: Louis A. Bedford Jr. and the Struggle for Equal Rights in Texas.* Dallas: Southern Methodist University Press, 2009.

Peter, Duane E. "The Freedman's Cemetery Project." In *Freedman's Cemetery: A Legacy of a Pioneer Black Community in Dallas, Texas,* edited by Duane E. Peter, Marsha Prior, Melissa M. Green, and Victoria G. Clow, 1-19. Plano: Geo-Marine, Inc., 2000.

Prior, Marsha and Robert V. Kemper, "From Freedman's Town to Uptown: Community Transformation and Gentrification in Dallas, Texas," *Urban Anthropology and Studies of Cultural Systems and World Economic Development* 34, no. 2/3 (Summer-Fall 2005). https://www.jstor.org/stable/40553482.

Quinn, Allen. "Central Boulevard Cost Toal Put at 18 Millions." *Dallas Morning News,* August 24, 1947.

Schulte, Terry Anne and Marsha Prior. "Epilogue." In *Freedman's Cemetery: A Legacy of a Pioneer Black Community in Dallas, Texas,* edited by Duane E. Peter, Marsha Prior, Melissa M. Green, and Victoria G. Clow, 191-196. Plano: Geo-Marine, Inc., 2000.

Smith, Thomas H. "African Americans in Dallas: From Slavery to Freedom." In *Dallas Reconsidered: Essays in Local History,* edited by Michael V. Hazel, 122-133. Dallas: Three Forks Press, 1995.

U.S. Census Bureau. "Characteristics of Housing by Census Tracts: 1950." 1950 Census of Housing: Volume 5 Block Statistics: Dallas, Texas, 1950, table 2. Accessed July 15, 2020. https://www.census.gov/library/publications/1953/dec/housing-vol-05.html.

Wilson, William H. "Adapting to Growth: Dallas, Texas and the Kessler Plan, 1908-1933." *Arizona and the West* 25, no. 3 (Autumn 1983). https://www.jstor.org/stable/40169230.

Deep Ellum Blues

Barr, Alwyn. *Black Texans: A History of African Americans in Texas, 1528-1995*. Norman: University of Oklahoma Press, 1996.

Biffle, Kent. "Freeway to Cut Fabled Street." *Dallas Morning News*, June 26, 1966.

Campbell, Randolph B. *Grass-Roots Reconstruction in Texas, 1865-1880*. Baton Rouge: Louisiana State University Press, 1997.

Coalition for a New Dallas. "I-345: Replace I-345 and Rebuild Dallas." Accessed November 10, 2020. https://www.coalitionforanewdallas.org/i-345.

Dallas Morning News, "Deep Ellum Extra Special," December 12, 1940.

Dallas Morning News, "Expressway Nears Completion," July 12, 1956.

Deep Ellum Foundation. *Deep Ellum Public Improvement District Strategic Plan*. Dallas: Deep Ellum Foundation, 2019.

Enstam, Elizabeth York, editor. *When Dallas Became a City: Letters of John Milton McCoy, 1870-1881*. Dallas: Dallas Historical Society, 1982, 46-47.

Govenar, Alan, and Jay Brakefield. *Deep Ellum: The Other Side of Dallas*. College Station: Texas A&M University Press, 2013.

Greene, A. C. *Dallas USA*. Austin: Texas Monthly Press, 1984.

Hostetter, Alaena. "Club Dada Celebrates 30 Years as Deep Ellum's Artistic Backbone." *Dallas Observer*, September 19, 2016. https://www.dallasobserver.com/music/club-dada-celebrates-30-years-as-deep-ellums-artistic-backbone-8715489.

McElhaney, Jackie. "From Oxen to Rails: The Development of Dallas as a Transportation Center." *Legacies: A History Journal for Dallas and North Central Texas* 7, no. 1 (Spring, 1995), 8-14. https://texashistory.unt.edu/ark:/67531/metapth35110/m1/10/. The Portal to Texas History.

Perry, Andre, Jonathan Rothwell, and David Harshbarger. *The Devaluation of Assets in Black Neighborhoods: The Case of Residential Property*. Washington, DC: The Brookings Institution, 2018.

Quinn, Allen. "Four-Level Grade Separation Considered for Expressways." *Dallas Morning News*, June 20, 1954.

Roark, Carol. "The Story of the Pythian Temple." *Legacies: A History Journal for Dallas and North Central Texas* 29, no. 1 (Spring 2017). https://texashistory.unt.edu/ark:/67531/metapth992892/m1/6/.

Roche, Bruce. "Latimer, James Wellington (1825-1859)." Texas State Historical Association Handbook of Texas. Accessed February 27, 2021. https://www.tshaonline.org/handbook/entries/latimer-james-wellington.

Texas State Historical Association Handbook of Texas. "John Jay Good." Accessed February 27, 2021. https://www.tshaonline.org/handbook/entries/good-john-jay.

Ward, William. "Hidden Nooks of Dallas' Black Belt." *Dallas Morning News*, November 29, 1925.

The Park Left Standing

Barta, Carolyn. "Residential Pocket Faces Uncertain Future." *Dallas Morning News*, May 24, 1970.

City of Dallas Neighborhood Designation Task Force. "Dallas Landmark Commission Landmark Nomination Form: Luna Tortilla Factory," August, 1995. https://dallascityhall.com/departments/sustainabledevelopment/historicpreservation/Pages/luna_tortilla_factory.aspx.

City of Dallas Neighborhood Designation Task Force. "Dallas Landmark Commission Landmark Nomination Form: St. Ann's School/St. Ann's Com. H. S. / Guadalupe Social Center,"

September 8, 1998. https://dallascityhall.com/departments/
sustainabledevelopment/historicpreservation/Pages/st_anns_
school.aspx.

City of Dallas Office of Historic Preservation. "Dallas Landmark
Structures and Sites: Pike Park." Accessed November 10, 2020.
https://dallascityhall.com/departments/sustainabledevelopment/
historicpreservation/Pages/Pike-Park.aspx.

Dallas Morning News. "Officials Jubilant at Approval Given Highway Projects." October 2, 1937.

Dallas Morning News. "Council Gets Tracts for Turney Route."
July 27, 1939.

Dallas Morning News. "Turney Street Connection." February 15, 1940.

Dallas Morning News. "Ribbon Road Barrier Snipped." October 15, 1941.

Dallas Morning News. "Community House Gets Repairs in Pike Park."
January 15, 1950.

Fairbanks, Robert B. The War on Slums in the Southwest: Public Housing and Slum Clearance in Texas, Arizona, and New
Mexico, 1935-1965. Philadelphia: Temple University Press, 2014.

Finklea, Robert. "Officer Suspended, Charged." Dallas Morning
News, July 25, 1973.

Greene, A. C. "Woman's Determination Shaped Tortilla Factory."
Dallas Morning News, July 7, 1991.

Jaramillo, Cassandra. "Dallas' Little Mexico Is Nearly Gone in
Uptown, but Here's What Remains." Dallas Morning News,
March 14, 2018. https://www.dallasnews.com/news/2018/03/14/
dallas-little-mexico-is-nearly-gone-in-uptown-but-heres-what-
remains/.

Montes, Geoff. "Preserving Latino History at Pike Park in Dallas."
National Trust for Historic Preservation. December 22, 2014.
https://savingplaces.org/stories/preserving-latino-history-
pike-park-dallas#.YEKOQOZMHOR.

Katy Railroad Historical Society. "Route Maps." Accessed September 1, 2020. https://katyrailroad.org/map/.

KERA. "Little Mexico: El Barrio (1997)." August 1, 2013. Video, 28:57. https://youtu.be/DFXH9q_av4s.

Limón, Elvia. "What's the History behind the Little Mexico Village Apartments in Uptown? Curious Texas Investigates." *Dallas Morning News*, January 9, 2019. https://www.dallasnews.com/news/curious-texas/2019/01/09/what-s-the-history-behind-the-little-mexico-village-apartments-in-uptown-curious-texas-investigates/.

Payne, Darwin. *Big D: Triumphs and Troubles of an American Supercity in the 20th Century.* Dallas: Three Forks Press, 1994.

Phillips, Michael. *White Metropolis: Race, Ethnicity, and Religion in Dallas, 1841-2001.* Austin: University of Texas Press, 2006.

Preziosi, David. "Lost + Found: Pike Park—Little Mexico's Struggle for its Oasis." *Columns Magazine,* Winter 2020.

Rice, Gwendolyn. "Little Mexico and the Barrios of Dallas." In *Dallas Reconsidered: Essays in Local History*, ed. Michael V. Hazel, 158-168. Dallas: Three Forks Press, 1995.

Simpson, Amy. *Pike Park: The Heart and History of Mexican Culture in Dallas.* Dallas: Los Barrios Unidos Community Clinic, 1981.

Slotboom, Oscar. *Dallas-Fort Worth Freeways: Texas-Sized Ambition.* Totowa, NJ: Lightning Press, 2014.

Smith, Jason Scott. *Building New Deal Liberalism: The Political Economy of Public Works, 1933-1956.* New York: Cambridge University Press, 2006.

St. Ann's Alumni & Friends of Little Mexico, Inc. "Home." Accessed November 5, 2020. http://www.stannsalumniofdallas.org/index.html.

Tatum, Henry. "Park's Identity Returned." *Dallas Morning News*, November 13, 1978.

Texas Historical Commission. "Dallas' Little Mexico." September 23, 2015. Video, 2:28. https://youtu.be/Aou8g1-B7BU.

Trujillo, Carol. "Dallas' First Barrio." *Dallas Morning News,* September 13, 1987.

Villasana, Sol. *Dallas's Little Mexico.* Charleston: Arcadia Publishing, 2011.

Williams, Roy H., and Kevin J. Shay. *Time Change: An Alternative View of the History of Dallas.* Dallas: To Be Publishing Co., 1991.

Wilonsky, Robert. "Farewell to 'the Last Remnants' of Dallas' Little Mexico, as Houses on Harry Hines, Harwood Await Demolition." *Dallas Morning News.* December 13, 2019. https://www.dallasnews.com/news/commentary/2019/12/13/farewell-to-the-last-remnants-of-dallas-little-mexico-as-buildings-on-harry-hines-harwood-await-demolition/.

A Neighborhood Disappearing Act

Adams Wade, Norma. "Trying to Preserve the Past—Area Residents Work to Save Neighborhood." *Dallas Morning News,* February 13, 1995.

Bcworkshop. *Neighborhood Stories: Tenth Street.* Dallas, TX: Bcworkshop, 2013. https://issuu.com/bcworkshop/docs/booklet_final_web.

Buildingcommunityworkshop. "Neighborhood Stories: Tenth Street." June 15, 2013. Video, 27:42. https://vimeo.com/68448526.

Black & Clark Funeral Home. "Our History." Accessed December 23, 2020. https://blackandclark.com/43/Our-History.html.

City of Dallas. "The Dallas City Code Section 51A-4.501(i) 'Certificate for Demolition for a Residential Structure with No More Than 3,000 Square Feet of Floor Area Pursuant to Court Order.'" American Legal Publishing Corporation. Accessed

March 26, 2021. https://codelibrary.amlegal.com/codes/dallas/latest/dallas_tx/0-0-0-36120.

City of Dallas Department of Planning and Development, *Planned Development District for the Tenth Street Neighborhood* (Dallas, TX: City of Dallas Department of Planning and Development, 1993), 7.

City of Dallas Office of Historic Preservation. "City of Dallas Demolition Delay Log." Demolition Delay Overlay Districts. Accessed October 1, 2020. https://docs.google.com/spread-sheets/d/1ao7QJK7ydyWnHyFmeAr1vFOiwGmpu6POrs_xzvSW-30/edit#gid=1111470644.

City Plan Commission. *An Outline of the Master Plan.* Dallas, TX: City of Dallas City Plan Commission, 1946. https://texashistory.unt.edu/ark:/67531/metapth752753/m1/79/, The Portal to Texas History.

Dallas Morning News. "Clarendon to Become Major Traffic Artery." April 25, 1940.

Erickson, Bethany. "Positive News, for Once, in Tenth Street Historic District." Candy's Dirt, May 30, 2019. https://candysdirt.com/2019/05/30/positive-news-for-once-in-tenth-street-historic-district/.

Gilliam, Terry, and Terry Jones. *Monty Python and the Holy Grail.* Python (Monty) Pictures, 1975. DVD, 1:32:00.

Hampton, Joanna and Robert Swann. "Tenth Street is Bleeding." *Columns*, Winter 2020. https://www.aiadallas.org/v/columns-detail/Tenth-Street-is-Bleeding/12g/.

The History Engine. "Texas Homestead Law and the Economic Depression of the 1890s." Accessed December 23, 2020. https://historyengine.richmond.edu/episodes/view/2392.

National Trust for Historic Preservation. "America's 11 Most Endangered Historic Places—Past Listings." Accessed October 1, 2020. https://savingplaces.org/11most-past-listings#. YF6k_-ZOnOR.

National Trust for Historic Preservation. "Discover America's 11 Most Endangered Historic Places for 2019." May 30, 2019. https://savingplaces.org/stories/11-most-endangered-historic-places-2019#.YF6ldeZOnOR.

Oak Cliff Cemetery. "History." Accessed December 23, 2020. https://www.oakcliffcemetery.org/history/.

Pace University Elisabeth Haub School of Law. "Non-Conforming Users." Accessed December 26, 2020. https://law.pace.edu/non-conforming-users.

Powell, Larry. "After Awhile, Playing the Heavy Wears a Little Thin." *Dallas Morning News*, March 14, 1995.

Rangel, Jennifer. "Dallas must focus on preserving the Tenth Street Historic District." North Dallas Gazette, June 19, 2019. https://northdallasgazette.com/2019/06/19/dallas-must-focus-on-preserving-the-tenth-street-historic-district/.

Slotboom, Oscar. *Dallas-Fort Worth Freeways: Texas-Sized Ambition*. Totowa, NJ: Lightning Press, 2014.

Stone, Rachel. "Architecture at Risk: Six Endangered Oak Cliff Places." Advocate Oak Cliff. Accessed December 23, 2020. https://oakcliff.advocatemag.com/2018/08/historic-architecture-at-risk/.

U.S. National Park Service, "National Register of Historic Places Registration Form: Tenth Street Historic District," June 17, 1994. https://catalog.archives.gov/id/40968740.

Wilonsky, Robert. "Dallas Eyes Ways to Spare the Historic Tenth Street District, Which Is Now on a National Most-Endangered List." *Dallas Morning News*, May 30, 2019. https://www.dallasnews.com/opinion/commentary/2019/05/30/dallas-eyes-ways-to-spare-the-historic-tenth-street-district-which-is-now-on-a-national-most-endangered-list/.

A Case For Reframing Our History

Lorde, Audre *The Selected Works of Audre Lorde*. Edited by Roxane Gay. New York: W. W. Norton & Company, 2020.

"Motor Killings and the Engineer" (editorial). *Engineering News Record* 89, November 9, 1922. https://archive.org/details/engineeringnewsr89newy/page/774/mode/2up.

National History Center. "Infrastructure Development." *C-SPAN*, May 4, 2018. Video, 1:01:48. https://www.c-span.org/video/?445036-1/history-professors-discuss-past-current-infrastructure-projects.

Norton, Peter. *Fighting Traffic: The Dawn of the Motor Age in the American City*. Cambridge: The MIT Press, 2008.

Space, Place, Justice

La Vigne, Nancy. "The Power of Language: Rethinking How We Talk about Place." *Urban Institute*. Accessed January 17, 2021. https://www.urban.org/debates/power-language-rethinking-how-we-talk-about-place.

Lee, Bryan. "America's Cities Were Designed to Oppress." Citylab. June 3, 2020. https://www.bloomberg.com/news/articles/2020-06-03/how-to-design-justice-into-america-s-cities.

Merriam-Webster. s.v. "transference (n.)." Accessed February 16, 2017. https://www.merriam-webster.com/dictionary/transference.

Mock, Brentin. "The Meaning of Blight." *Citylab*. February 16, 2017. https://www.bloomberg.com/news/articles/2017-02-16/why-we-talk-about-urban-blight.

Moore, Justin Garrett. "Why We Need a New Word for 'Blight'." Medium. October 8, 2015. https://medium.com/@jgmoore/why-we-need-a-new-word-for-blight-52a65fbf1b73#.pko74m5zt.

Okun, Tema. *White Supremacy Culture.* dRworks, n.d. https://www.dismantlingracism.org/white-supremacy-culture. html.

Schilling, Joseph, and Jimena Pinzon. *Charting the Multiple Meanings of Blight: A National Literature Review on Addressing the Community Impacts of Blighted Properties.* Blacksburg, VA: 2015.

Spievack, Natalie, and Cameron Okeke. "How We Should Talk about Racial Disparities." Urban Wire: Race and Ethnicity. February 26, 2020. https://www.urban.org/urban-wire/how-we-should-talk-about-racial-disparities.

TEDx Talks. "Race, Architecture, and Tales for the Hood l Bryan Lee l TEDxTU." April 22, 2016. Video, 9:13. https://youtu.be/ gfg3IB7i24.

The Detroit News. "Craig L. Wilkins on Hip Hop Culture and Architecture." Facebook. October 22, 2017. https://www.facebook.com/ watch/?v=10155054427073857.

Wilkins, Craig L. *The Aesthetics of Equity: Notes on Race, Space, Architecture, and Music.* Minneapolis: University of Minnesota Press, 2007.

Vey, Jennifer S., and Hannah Love, "Recognizing That Words Have the Power to Harm, We Commit to Using More Just Language to Describe Places," *Brookings,* July 13, 2020. https://www.brookings.edu/blog/the-avenue/2020/07/13/ recognizing-that-words-have-the-power-to-harm-we-commit-to-using-more-just-language-to-describe-places/.

Pattern For A Just City

Alexander, Christopher, Sara Ishikawa, and Murray Silverstein. *A Pattern Language: Towns, Buildings, Construction.* New York: Oxford University Press, 1977.

Barrett, Peter, Yufan Zhang, Fay Davies, and Lucinda Barrett. *Clever Classrooms: Summary and Report of the HEAD Project.* Manchester: University of Salford, 2015. http://usir.salford.ac.uk/id/eprint/35221.

Bernstein, Fred A. "Can This Planner Save Detroit?" Architect, October 6, 2010. https://www.architectmagazine.com/design/urbanism-planning/can-this-planner-save-detroit_o.

Griffin, Toni. "A New Vision For Rebuilding Detroit." Filmed September 2013 in New York, New York. TED video, 11:37. https://www.ted.com/talks/toni_griffin_a_new_vision_for_rebuilding_detroit?language=en.

Griffin, Toni, Laura Greenberg, Laier-Rayshon Smith, ed. *Patterned Justice: Design Language for a Just Pittsburgh.* Cambridge: Just City Lab at Harvard Graduate School of Design, 2020.

Griffin, Toni. "Designing Cities for Justice With Toni Griffin, 'Patterned Justice' Co-Editor & Harvard's Just City Lab Lead Innovator." September 22, 2020, in *We Can Be* produced by Grant Oliphant. Podcast, MP3 audio, 32:18. https://www.heinz.org/podcast.

The Just City Lab. *Just City Index.* New York: The Just City Lab, 2017. https://www.designforthejustcity.org/engage.

Merrill, Stephen. "Flexible Classrooms: Research Is Scarce, but Promising." Edutopia. June 14, 2018. https://www.edutopia.org/article/flexible-classrooms-research-scarce-promising.

Montoya, Regina, and Mark Clayton. "Mayor's Task Force on Poverty Update." PowerPoint presentation, presented to City of Dallas Human and Social Needs Committee, May 7, 2018. https://dallascityhall.com/government/Council%20Meeting%20Documents/hsn_2_mayor%E2%80%99s-task-force-on-poverty-update_combined_050718.pdf.

A Community Vision

Arnstein, Sherry. "A Ladder of Citizen Participation." *Journal of the American Planning Association* 85, no 1 (2019): 24-34. https://doi.org/10.1080/01944363.2018.1559388.

Brown Wilson, Barbara. *Resilience for All: Striving for Equity through Community-Driven Design.* Washington, D.C.: Island Press, 2018).

Blue Star Recycling. "Blue Star Recycling Dallas Facility." August 29, 2017. Video, 9:40. https://youtu.be/9Ch3bSnovsg.

The Catalyst. "Growing the Economy—Inclusively." Fall 2019. https://www.bushcenter.org/catalyst/capitalism/parker-myers-growing-the-economy-inclusively.html.

City of Dallas. "Former Blue Star Recycling Cleanup." Accessed February 18, 2021. https://storymaps.arcgis.com/stories/0a10210bd0924f1e96774834c6foeda2.

City of Dallas. "ForwardDallas Comprehensive Land Use Plan Update—About." Accessed January 30, 2021. https://dallascityhall.com/departments/pnv/Forward-Dallas/Pages/about.aspx.

Cooper, Brooklynn. "Dallas City Council Approves $450,000 Bid to Clean up Shingle Mountain." *Dallas Morning News*, October 13, 2020. https://www.dallasnews.com/news/environment/2020/10/13/dallas-city-council-approves-450000-bid-to-clean-up-shingle-mountain/.

Dallas Peace & Justice Center. "Outstanding New Activist Organization: Southern Sector Rising." Accessed February 15, 2021. https://www.dpjc.org/outstanding-new-activist-organization-southern-sector-rising.

Data USA. "Data USA: Dallas, TX." Accessed March 18, 2021. https://datausa.io/profile/geo/dallas-tx/#demographics.

Downwinders at Risk. "Toxic Shingle Mountain: Blue Star Recycling's Environmental Crisis in South Dallas." March 19, 2019. Video, 4:45. https://youtu.be/5QmhmBOAwwE.

Floral Farms Neighborhood Plan. (Dallas, TX: Neighbors United/ Vecinos Unidos & Southern Dallas Neighborhood Self Defense Project, 2020). https://southerndallasneighborhooddefense.wordpress.com/ floral-farms/.

Goodman, Matt. "The Reality TV Twin Who Built Shingle Mountain." *D Magazine*, August 2019. https://www.dmagazine.com/ publications/d-magazine/2019/august/chris-ganter-southern-dallas-shingle-mountain/.

Jackson, Marsha. "Every Level of Government Failed Southern Dallas by Allowing Shingle Mountain to Grow." *Dallas Morning News*, April 2, 2019. https://www.dallasnews.com/opinion/ commentary/2019/04/02/every-level-of-government-failed-southern-dallas-by-allowing-shingle-mountain-to-grow/.

Kevin Krause, Kevin, and Carrington Tatum. "City of Dallas Seeks Contractor to Clean up Shingle Mountain." *Dallas Morning News*, September 10, 2020. https://www.dallasnews.com/news/ politics/2020/09/10/city-of-dallas-seeks-bids-to-clean-up-toxic-shingle-mountain/.

Mayo, Evelyn, Emily Worland, Elizabeth Weis, and Jackson Cole. *In Plain Sight: Industrial Compliance Issues in Southern Dallas.* Dallas: Legal Aid of Northwest Texas, 2019.

Merck, Amanda. "Jennifer Rangel: Creating Bilingual Cartoons to Teach Zoning 101." Salud America!, December 12, 2020. https://salud-america.org/jennifer-rangel-creating-bilingual-cartoons-to-teach-zoning-101/.

Rangel, Jennifer. "Geographical Examination of Latino Urbanism: Oak Cliff as a Case Study." (master's thesis, UNC Chapel Hill, 2018). 36-44. https://doi.org/10.17615/5xhw-bj19.

Rangel, Jennifer. "Neighborhood Equity and Latino Urbanism in Dallas, TX." Interview by Demetria McCain, *Inclusive Communities Project*, Storycorp, June 15, 2018. Audio, 31:22. https://archive.storycorps.org/interviews/neighborhood-equity-and-latino-urbanism-in-dallas-tx/.

Rangel, Jennifer. "Question Your Surroundings." *Visible Magazine*, May 8, 2019. https://visiblemagazine.com/question-your-surroundings/.

Southern Dallas Neighborhood Self Defense Project. "Floral Farms." Accessed January 27, 2021. https://southerndallasneighborhooddefense.wordpress.com/floral-farms/.

Southern Dallas Neighborhood Self Defense Project. "Home." Accessed January 27, 2021. https://southerndallasneighborhooddefense.wordpress.com/.

Southern Sector Rising. "Stand with Marsha. Move the Mountain." Accessed February 15, 2021. https://southernsectorrising.org/move-the-mountain/.

Tatum, Carrington. "In Mock Trials, Protesters Find Dallas Officials Guilty of 'Monstrous Neglect' over Shingle Mountain." *Dallas Morning News*, August 29, 2020. https://www.dallasnews.com/news/environment/2020/08/29/in-mock-trials-protesters-find-dallas-officials-guilty-of-monstrous-neglect-over-shingle-mountain/.

Tatum, Carrington. "What You Need to Know about Shingle Mountain's Complex History in Southern Dallas." *Dallas Morning News*, September 17, 2020. https://www.dallasnews.com/news/2020/09/17/timeline-shingle-mountains-complex-history-in-oak-cliff/.

U.S. Census Bureau. "QuickFacts: Dallas City Texas." Accessed January 30, 2021. https://www.census.gov/quickfacts/fact/table/dallascitytexas/RHI725219#RHI725219.

U.S. Environmental Protection Agency, U.S. EPA Innovations Workgroup, *Environmental Issues Associated with Asphalt Shingle Recycling*, by Timothy Townsend, John Powell, and Chad Xu. Gainesville, Florida, 2007.

Wilonsky, Robert. "'It's Unacceptable': Why a Dallas Woman Lives Next to Mountains of Ground-up Shingles." *Dallas Morning News*, December 13, 2018. https://www.dallasnews.com/opinion/commentary/2018/12/13/it-s-unacceptable-why-a-dallas-woman-lives-next-to-mountains-of-ground-up-shingles/.

Wilonsky, Robert. "Shingle Mountain Fight Came to City Hall, Just as Dallas Moved to Shut down Asphalt Recycler." *Dallas Morning News*, March 20, 2019. https://www.dallasnews.com/news/politics/2019/03/20/shingle-mountain-fight-came-to-city-hall-just-as-dallas-moved-to-shut-down-asphalt-recycler/.

The "G" Word

Brey, Jared. "Study Suggests Gentrification Has an Upside. Housing Advocates Aren't Yet Convinced." Next City, July 25, 2019. https://nextcity.org/daily/entry/study-suggests-gentrification-has-an-upside-housing-advocates-not-convinced.

Metro Dallas Homeless Alliance. *2020 Dallas and Collin Counties Point in Time Homeless Count Results—Summary*. Dallas, TX: Metro Dallas Homeless Alliance, 2020. http://www.mdhadallas.org/homeless-pit-count/.

Mitchell, Keri. "Does the Fate of West Dallas Rest on a 400-Foot Tower Next to la Bajada?" *Dallas Free Press*, December 16, 2020. https://dallasfreepress.com/west-dallas/does-the-fate-of-west-dallas-rest-on-a-400-foot-tower-next-to-la-bajada/.

Ogbu, Liz. "What If Gentrification Was about Healing Communities Rather Than Displacing Them?" Filmed November 2017 at TED-

Women, New Orleans, LA. Video, 14:54. https://www.ted.com/
talks/liz_ogbu_what_if_gentrification_was_about_healing_
communities_instead_of_displacing_them?language=en.

Simek, Peter. "Trinity Groves: The New Dallas Starts Here." *D Magazine*, January 2013. https://www.dmagazine.com/publications/
d-magazine/2013/january/trinity-groves-the-new-dallas-
starts-here/.

Simek, Peter. "New Study Shows Gentrification May Not Be the
Boogeyman Many Fear." *D Magazine*, July 19, 2019.
https://www.dmagazine.com/frontburner/2019/07/new-study-
shows-gentrification-may-not-be-the-boogeyman-many-fear/.

U.S. Federal Reserve. Federal Reserve Bank of Philadelphia. *The
Effects of Gentrification on the Well-Being and Opportunity of
Original Resident Adults and Children*, by Quentin Brummet,
and Davin Reed. Philadelphia, Pennsylvania, 2019.
https://www.philadelphiafed.org/community-development/
housing-and-neighborhoods/the-effects-of-gentrification-on-
the-well-being-and-opportunity-of-original-resident.

Way, Heather, Elizabeth Muller, and Jake Wegman. *Uprooted: Residential Displacement in Austin's Gentrifying Neighborhoods
and What Can Be Done about It*. Austin, TX: University of
Texas at Austin Center for Sustainable Development, 2018.
https://sites.utexas.edu/gentrificationproject/..austin-uprooted-
report-maps/.

Reinvesting In Development

Anderson, Monte. "Monte Anderson on Incremental Development." Interview by Kevin Shepherd. *Go Cultivate!*, Verdunity,
December 21, 2018. Audio, 58:08. https://www.verdunity.com/
podcast/episode-18.

Avery, Derek, Bianca Avery. "Can You Have Revitalization Without Gentrification? With Bianca & Derek Avery." Interview by Jordan Clark. *Go Cultivate!*, Verdunity, March 14, 2019. Audio, 34:00. https://www.verdunity.com/podcast/episode-29.

Avery, Derek. "Revitalization Without Gentrification—With Derek Avery." Interview by Ryan Short. *Eyes on the Street,* CivicBrand, May 12, 2020. Audio, 10:55. https://www.civicbrand.com/insights/podcasts/revitalization-without-gentrification-with-derek-avery.

Board of Governors of the Federal Reserve System. "Community Reinvestment Act (CRA)." Last updated September 28, 2020. Accessed February 7, 2021. https://www.federalreserve.gov/consumerscommunities/cra_about.htm.

Byron, Audrey. "Can You Have Revitalization Without Gentrification? Derek Avery Thinks So." Strong Towns, October 23, 2018. https://www.strongtowns.org/journal/2018/10/22/can-you-have-revitalization-without-gentrification-derek-avery-thinks-so.

COIR Holdings. "Our People." Accessed November 2, 2020. http://www.derekandbianca.com/about.

Curren, Ryan, Nora Liu, Dwayne Marsh, and Kalima Rose. *Equitable Development as a Tool to Advance Racial Equity.* (Chapel Hill, NC: The Local & Regional Government Alliance on Race and Equity, 2015). https://www.racialequityalliance.org/resources/equitable-development-tool-advance-racial-equity/.

Incremental Development Alliance. "Home." Accessed November 2, 2020. https://www.incrementaldevelopment.org/.

Incremental Development Alliance. "Our Work." Accessed February 6, 2021. https://www.incrementaldevelopment.org/work.

Jensen, Jeremiah. "Developer Monte Anderson Wants To Stop the Handouts." *D CEO,* December 2018. https://www.dmagazine.com/publications/d-ceo/2018/december/developer-monte-anderson-wants-to-stop-the-handouts/.

Meeks, Tomiko. "Freedman's Town: A Lesson in the Failure of Historic Preservation." *Houston History Magazine* 8 (no. 1, 2011), 42-44. https://houstonhistorymagazine.org/2011/04/freedmans-town-a-lesson-in-the-failure-of-historic-preservation/.

Schechter, David, Jason Trahan, Chance Horner, and T. Nicole Waivers. "'They Underestimate What We Can Do': WFAA Finds Banks Exclude Blacks, Hispanics in Southern Dallas From Access to Loans." WFAA-TV, November 22, 2020. https://www.wfaa.com/article/news/local/investigates/banking-below-30-southern-dallas-cut-off-by-freeway-also-left-off-banking-maps/287-10557dd3-bbf4-44a2-b786-44c6347a6e48.

Schutze, Jim. "One Dallas Developer's Secret: Bigger Isn't Always Better." *D Magazine*, November 2020. https://www.dmagazine.com/publications/d-magazine/2020/november/one-dallas-developers-secret-bigger-isnt-always-better/?ref=mpw.

Wilonsky, Robert. "City Hall Offered $3m To Open a Grocery Store in a Southern Dallas Food Desert and Got No Takers." *The Dallas Morning News,* November 30, 2016. https://www.dallasnews.com/news/politics/2016/11/30/city-hall-offered-3m-to-open-a-grocery-store-in-a-southern-dallas-food-desert-and-got-no-takers/.

Wood, Roger. *Down in Houston: Bayou City Blues.* (Austin, TX: University of Texas Press, 2003).

A Diversity Of Actors

African Burial Ground National Monument. "History & Culture." April 26, 2019. https://www.nps.gov/afbg/learn/historyculture/index.htm.

American Institute of Architects. "Architect Pascale Sablan Honored
With 2021 Whitney M. Yound Jr. Award." American Institute
of Architects press release, December 9, 2020. American Institute of Architects website. https://www.aia.org/press-releases/
6355475-architect-pascale-sablan-honored-with-2021, accessed
December 27, 2020.

Archer, Diane, and David Dodman. 2015. "Making Capacity Building Critical: Power and Justice in Building Urban Climate
Resilience in Indonesia and Thailand." Urban Climate, 14 (1),
68-78. https://doi.org/10.1016/j.uclim.2015.06.007.

Beyond the Built Environment. "Great Diverse Designers Library."
Accessed December 31, 2020. https://www.beyondthebuilt.com/
great-designer-library-state.

Beyond the Built Environment. "Home." Accessed December 28,
2020. https://www.beyondthebuilt.com/.

Burke, Amy. Science and Engineering Labor Force. Science & Engineering Indicators. Alexandria, VA: National Science Board,
2019. https://ncses.nsf.gov/pubs/nsb20198/demographic-trends-
of-the-s-e-workforce.

Columbia GSAPP. "Bryan C. Lee, Jr. 2020." September 28, 2020.
Video, 1:32:18. https://youtu.be/-FsQSYzJAsQ.

Creative Reaction Lab. Equity-Centered Community Design Field
Guide. St. Louis, MO: Creative Reaction Lab, 2018.

Data USA. "Architects, Except Naval." Accessed December 29,
2020. https://datausa.io/profile/soc/architects-except-naval.

Data USA. "Urban & Regional Planners." Accessed December 29,
2020. https://datausa.io/profile/soc/urban-regional-planners.

Elese, Maya. "Knowledge Session: The Griot Tradition." I Am Hip
Hop Magazine, March 18, 2018. https://www.abhmuseum.org/
about/what-is-griot/.

Fazzare, Elizabeth. "Architect-Advocate Pascale Sablan Is Revising the History of the Built Environment." Forbes. September 26, 2020. https://www.noma.net/about-noma/.

Kaplan, Fran. "What Is a Griot?" America's Black Holocaust Museum. Accessed December 29, 2020. https://www.abhmuseum.org/about/what-is-griot/.

LinkedIn. "Pascale Sablan FAIA, NOMA, LEED AP." Accessed December 30, 2020. https://www.linkedin.com/in/pascale-sablan-faia-noma-leed-ap-a0331979/.

Matera, Sonia. "The Role of Power Dynamics for Community Engagement: A Case Study in Myanmar." Masters Thesis, Sweden: LUND University, 2020. http://lup.lub.lu.se/student-papers/record/9016018.

McLeod, Saul. "Albert Bandura's Social Learning Theory." *Simply Psychology*. Accessed January 15, 2021. https://www.simplypsychology.org/bandura.html.

NOMA Louisiana. "Project Pipeline." Accessed December 26, 2020. http://www.nomala.org/project-pipeline.

Rao, Anjulie. "Stand Up and Stand Out." *Landscape Architect Magazine,* May 2020. https://landscapearchitecturemagazine.org/2020/05/28/stand-up-and-stand-out/.

Sablan, Pascale. "Redesign a School." Presented at the Brooklyn Vol. 4 "Brooklyn Vol. 4—Design Week," Brooklyn, NY, May 18, 2015. https://www.pechakucha.com/presentations/redesign-a-school-2.

Schaerer, Michael, Christilene du Pleiss, Andy J. Yap, and Stefan Thau. "Low Power Individuals in Social Power Research: A Quantitative Review, Theoretical Framework, and Empirical Test." *Organizational Behavior and Human Decision Making,* 149 (November 2018): 73-96. https://doi.org/10.1016/j.obhdp.2018.08.004.

Taylor, Jessie. "In Conversation With: Valerie Franklin." Nashville
   Design Week 2020. Accessed December 28, 2020.
   https://nashvilledesignweek.org/conversations/valarie-franklin.

Paving A New Way

Urban Institute. "Keynote Address from Rev. Starsky Wilson, President and CEO of Children's Defense Fund." January 19, 2021.
   Video, 18:56. https://youtu.be/VID4OrF4ll8.